Jean Bowring's
Appetisers, Soups & Entrees

Jean Bowring's

Appetisers, Soups & Entrees

ANGUS & ROBERTSON

Photography by Gary Isaacs

Angus & Robertson Publishers
London · Sydney · Melbourne · Singapore
Manila

First published by Angus & Robertson Publishers, Australia,
1978

© Jean Bowring 1978

National Library of Australia
Cataloguing-in-publication data.
Bowring, Jean.
    Jean Bowring's appetisers, soups & entrees.
    Index
    ISBN 0 207 13651 3.
    1. Cookery (Appetizers). 2. Soups. 3. Cookery (Entrees).
    I. Title. II. Title: Appetisers, soups & entrees
641 · 812

Typeset in Monophoto Bembo by
Asco Trade Typesetting Limited, Hong Kong
Printed in Hong Kong

FOREWORD

I hope you will enjoy this collection of recipes—favourites from The Jean Bowring Cookbook *plus many new and different dishes. All the recipes have been set out clearly, with easy-to-follow directions, so that, with care, every cook can achieve perfect results every time. Please remember to read through the recipe before beginning, so that you know which ingredients and utensils you are going to need, and what you have to do. This will help you to work efficiently. Weigh and measure exactly—never try to guess quantities—and follow the method closely. Then you can be sure of success, for every one of these recipes has been well tested in my own kitchen.*

Good cooking, good entertaining—and good eating!

CONTENTS

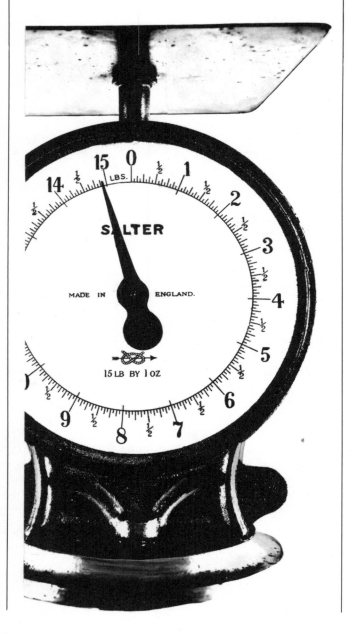

WEIGHING & MEASURING

Successful cooking depends on accurate measuring of ingredients. You have the choice of scales, cups and spoons.

The newer scales on the market will give the weight in grams, the older ones in ounces and pounds. To cater for both we've set out the conversion scale recommended by the Metric Conversion Board for weights which are now referred to as "masses", and in all recipes give you both the **metric** expressed in grams and kilograms and the **imperial** in ounces and pounds.

Should your choice be for cup measurements remember to use the standard metric cup.

If you are measuring in spoons, use the standard metric tablespoon and teaspoon. The dessertspoon has been dropped from the metric system of measuring ingredients for cooking.

All measurements, whether they are cup or spoon are level unless otherwise stated.

When making spoon measurements take a spoonful and level it off with the blade of a knife. For half a spoonful divide the ingredients by running the knife lengthwise down the centre.

For cup measurements place the cup on a flat surface and spoon or pour the ingredient in. Never dip a cup into a soft ingredient such as flour. This could lead to over measurement as the flour would be packed down. As a general rule the only ingredient to be firmly packed in a cup is brown sugar.

Butter or other shortenings are difficult to measure by cup and for this reason recipes in this book are given in kilograms or grams *and* pounds or ounces.

Many of the well known brands of butter have cutting lines marked on the wrapping indicating grams. It is easy, too, to cut a pack of butter into four equal portions when the recipe calls for that quantity.

Here is a simple conversion of ounces and pounds to metric grams and kilograms. Although the exact number of grams is slightly less than the 500 used here, to make calculations easier 30 grams represents one ounce and 500 grams one pound.

The spoon and cup measurement chart on page 10 will help those without scales.

LENGTH MEASUREMENT

The dimension of the cooking utensil and the thickness of dough or biscuit mixture is frequently given in a recipe and you'll need to know the conversion from inches to centimetres or millimetres.

The table follows:

LENGTH MEASUREMENT CONVERSION

In	mm	cm
$\frac{1}{16}$	2	—
$\frac{1}{8}$	3	—
$\frac{1}{4}$	5	—
$\frac{1}{2}$	10	1
$\frac{3}{4}$	20	2
1	25	2.5
$1\frac{1}{2}$		4
2		5
$2\frac{1}{2}$		6
3		8
4		10
5		12
6		15
7		18
8		20
9		23
10		25
12		30
14		35
16		40
18		45
20		50

WEIGHT MEASUREMENT

CONVERSION OF MASSES (WEIGHT)

Avoirdupois		Metric
$\frac{1}{2}$ oz	is replaced by	15 g
1 oz		30 g
2 oz		60 g
3 oz		90 g
4 oz ($\frac{1}{4}$ lb)		125 g
5 oz		155 g
6 oz		185 g
7 oz		220 g
8 oz ($\frac{1}{2}$ lb)		250 g
9 oz		280 g
10 oz		315 g
11 oz		345 g
12 oz ($\frac{3}{4}$ lb)		375 g
13 oz		410 g
14 oz		440 g
15 oz		470 g
16 oz (1 lb)		500 g (0.5 kg)
24 oz ($1\frac{1}{2}$ lb)		750 g
32 oz (2 lb)		1000 g (1 kg)
3 lb		1500 g (1.5 kg)
4 lb		2000 g (2 kg)

LIQUID MEASURES

Liquid measures in this book are based on the standard measuring cup. This represents eight fluid ounces or 250 ml.

There are two and a half cups in one imperial pint.

The standard tablespoon measures 20 ml and the standard teaspoon 5 ml.

OVEN TEMPERATURES

The oven temperature is a most important part of baking. It is useless spending time, energy and good ingredients in making up a recipe only to see it ruined by either under or over cooking.

If you have an instruction book supplied by the manufacturer of your cooker, study it carefully. It will guide you on positions in the oven and in times for preheating.

Actual cooking temperatures I find remain the same regardless of the make of cooker or the type of fuel used. Metric conversion may pose a few difficulties if you have one of the older type cookers with fahrenheit readings on the thermostat. To overcome this I have given both celsius and fahrenheit in all recipes requiring oven cooking.

When it is a matter of a "moderate", "hot" or "slow" oven I use the following scale:

250° to 325° F or 120° to 160° C   slow oven

325° to 400° F or 160° to 200° C   moderate oven

400° to 450° F or 200° to 230° C   hot oven

450° to 500° F or 230° to 260° C   very hot oven

Broadly speaking the new celsius degrees are about half the degrees fahrenheit and here is the full range of baking temperatures you are likely to require for general baking:

TEMPERATURE CONVERSION FROM FAHRENHEIT TO CELSIUS

Thermostat setting °F	Thermostat setting °C
140	60
175	80
200	100
225	110
250	120
275	140
300	150
325	160
350	180
375	190
400	200
425	220
450	230
475	250
500	260

SPOON AND CUP MEASUREMENTS

1 level tablespoon = 30 g (1 oz) *of*	butter golden syrup honey lard margarine fat
1½ level tablespoons = 30 g (1 oz) *of*	barley gelatine rice sugar
2 level tablespoons = 30 g (1 oz) *of*	cocoa cornflour currants custard powder flour icing sugar sago sultanas
1 measuring cup = 60–90 g (2–3 oz) *of*	bread- crumbs (soft white) coconut suet (finely grated)

1 measuring cup = 125 g (4 oz) *of*	flour
	icing
	   sugar
	ground
	   nuts
	currants
	cocoa

1 measuring cup = 155 g (5 oz) *of*	peel (chopped) rice (ground) sugar (brown, loosely packed) sultanas
1 measuring cup = 185 g (6 oz) *of*	dates (chopped) sago sugar (brown, firmly packed) tapioca
1 measuring cup = 220 g (7 oz) *of*	rice
1 measuring cup = 250 g (8 oz) *of*	butter lard margarine

1 measuring cup = 375 g (12 oz) *of*	honey *or* golden syrup
2 measuring cups = 500 g (16 oz) *of*	liquid
2½ measuring cups = 500 ml (1 pt) *of*	liquid

COLD SAVOURIES

Just about everybody loves savouries, those pleasant and so versatile little titbits that suit almost any occasion— from the cocktail party through a quiet card evening to one of those get togethers that happen for no reason at all.

It's easy to stick a smoked oyster on a cracker biscuit, or a slice of cheese topped off with a gherkin, or a slice of hard boiled egg with a bit of tomato and parsley . . . so easy that just about everybody does it. But why not pay your guests the compliment of spending a little time on the preparation and presentation of your savouries.

Here is a good selection of cold savouries. Remember that if you have the time it is a good idea to provide a selection of both hot and cold hors d'œvres. Some delicious hot savouries are given in the next chapter.

ASPARAGUS HAM ROLLS

Asparagus pieces
French dressing
Ham
Cocktail picks

Toss 25 mm (1 in) pieces of well-drained asparagus in French dressing. Roll a strip of ham slightly narrower than the asparagus around each piece, securing with cocktail picks. Serve cold.

CELERY STUFFED WITH SARDINES

1 can sardines
1 cup mashed potato
1 teaspoon lemon juice
$\frac{1}{2}$ teaspoon Worcestershire sauce
1 teaspoon prepared mustard
1 teaspoon mayonnaise
$\frac{1}{2}$ teaspoon garlic salt
Pinch sugar
Celery stalks cut into 9 cm ($3\frac{1}{2}$ in) pieces

Garnish: chives *or* parsley, chopped

Drain the oil from the sardines and mash them with a fork. Add the mashed potato, lemon juice, Worcestershire sauce, mustard, mayonnaise, garlic salt and sugar.
Crisp the pieces of celery by soaking them in iced water. Before serving, wipe them dry and fill with the sardine mixture. Sprinkle with the chopped chives or parsley.

MINTED PINEAPPLE

Pinapple, canned *or* fresh
Cream cheese
Mint, chopped finely
Cocktail picks

Roll chunky pieces of canned or fresh pineapple in softened cream cheese, then toss in very finely chopped mint. Serve on cocktail picks.

FRESH MUSHROOM SAVOURIES

Mushrooms
French dressing
Meat paste *or* Speedy Pâté (p. 29)
Bacon

Select some small, slightly opened mushrooms. Wipe with a damp cloth and remove the stems (save the stems, they can be used in a casserole). Sprinkle the undersides of the mushrooms with French dressing, cover and let stand for at least one hour.
Now take some meat paste (or some Speedy Pâté p. 29), and spread on the undersides of the mushrooms. Roll tiny pieces of bacon on toothpicks, grill until the fat is clear and allow to cool. Impail the bacon rolls with toothpicks and press one into each mushroom. Serve cold.

SALAMI CUBES

Cream cheese
Salami, cubed
Parsley, chopped finely
Cocktail picks

Spread softened cream cheese on 1 cm ($\frac{1}{2}$ in) cubes of salami or other prepared or canned meat. Roll each cube in finely chopped parsley and serve on cocktail picks.

SAUSAGE WEDGES

2 cups mashed potato
1 tablespoon mayonnaise *or* prepared horseradish
$\frac{1}{2}$ cup grated cheese
Pinch cayenne pepper
1 tablespoon chopped gherkin
Salt
8 slices Continental sausage about 12 cm (5 in) in diameter and less than 5 mm ($\frac{1}{4}$ in) thick

Combine the potato, mayonnaise or horseradish, cheese, cayenne and gherkin, adding salt to taste. Spread one slice of the sausage with a thick coating of the mixture and top with another slice of sausage.

Repeat these layers twice, finishing with sausage: you will have four layers of sausage and three of filling. Press firmly together and wrap in waxed paper. Repeat with the remaining sausage and filling. Store in a cold part of the refrigerator but do not freeze.
Before serving, cut into slender pie-shaped wedges, using a sharp, thin-bladed knife (wipe the blade with a damp cloth each time you cut a slice). Arrange the wedges on a platter, laying them on their sides.

CAVIARE CANAPÉS 1.

12 rounds bread about 5 cm (2 in) in diameter
Hot oil for frying
2 hard-boiled eggs
Salt and peper
Paprika
1 teaspoon finely chopped parsley
1 teaspoon finely minced onion
60 g (2 oz) can of caviare
1 lemon

Garnish : small sprigs of parsley

Fry the bread rounds in the hot oil until golden brown on both sides. Drain on paper.
Remove the yolks from the hard-boiled eggs and press through a fine sieve, then season with salt, pepper and paprika. Finely chop the whites and season in the same way, adding the chopped parsley.
Spread each round of fried bread with egg-white mixture, then make a border with sieved egg yolk. Place some of the minced onion in the centre of each round, top with a little caviare and sprinkle the whole with lemon juice.
Decorate each canapé with a sprig of parsley. Serve cold.

CAVIARE CANAPÉS 2.

Red or black caviare
1 hard-boiled egg
Melba toast
Lemon *or* lime wedges
White onion *or* chives, chopped finely

Chill the caviare and place in a small container in the centre of your platter. Arrange small bowls of the chopped hard-boiled egg white, sieved hard-boiled egg yolk and either chopped onion or chives. Accompany with the Melba toast.
Guests spread the caviare on the toast and add a squeeze of lemon or lime then make their own choice of the egg, onion or chives.

CHEESE BALLS

1 125 g (4 oz) packet cream cheese
Chives *or* shallots, chopped
Carrot *or* parsley *or* nuts, chopped finely

Combine cream cheese with enough chopped chives or shallots to flavour. Take teaspoonsful of the mixture and roll into small balls.
Have ready either the grated carrot, chopped parsley or finely chopped nuts in which to roll the balls until covered. Chill until required.

CHEESE BUTTERFLIES

1 cup plain flour
Good pinch salt
Pinch cayenne pepper
$\frac{1}{2}$ level teaspoon dry mustard
60 g (2 oz) butter *or* margarine
30 g (1 oz) grated cheese
1 egg yolk
2 tablespoons milk
Lemon juice

Filling

2 tablespoons grated cheese
1 hard-boiled egg, chopped finely
Pinch each salt, cayenne pepper and mustard
1 tablespoon mayonnaise

Garnish: strips of gherkin

Sift the flour, salt, cayenne and mustard. Rub in the butter or margarine and add the grated cheese. Beat the egg yolk with the milk and lemon juice and stir into the mixture, making a fairly firm dough. Turn on to a lightly floured board and knead only until smooth on the outside. Roll thinly and cut into rounds with a 4 cm (1$\frac{1}{2}$ in) cutter. Place on a greased shallow oven tray and bake in a hot oven, 220° C (425° F), for about 10 minutes or until lightly browned. Allow to cool.

Combine the four ingredients for the filling, mixing well. Spread half the baked cheese rounds with this mixture. Cut the remaining rounds in halves and arrange them on top of the filling to resemble the wings of a butterfly. Place a strip of gherkin down the centre of each to represent the body, and attach two small narrow pieces of gherkin for the feelers. Serve cold.

CHEESE STRAWS

1$\frac{1}{4}$ cups plain flour
Pinch cayenne pepper
1 level teaspoon dry mustard
$\frac{1}{2}$ level teaspoon salt
125 g (4 oz) butter
1$\frac{1}{2}$ cups grated cheese
1 egg yolk
2 tablespoons cold water
Good squeeze lemon juice

Garnish: sprigs of parsley

Sift the flour, cayenne, mustard and salt. Rub in the butter and add the grated cheese. Beat the egg yolk with the water and lemon juice and add to the dry ingredients, making a rather firm dough.
Turn on to a lightly floured board and knead only until smooth. Roll 3 mm ($\frac{1}{8}$ in) thick and cut into strips 10 cm (4 in) long and 5 mm ($\frac{1}{4}$ in) wide. Place on a greased slide and bake in a moderate oven, 180° C (350° F), for about 12 minutes, or until a pale straw colour. Re-roll the scraps of pastry and cut a number of rings. Use a round cutter about 4 cm (1$\frac{1}{2}$ in) in diameter and a smaller one 2 cm ($\frac{3}{4}$ in) in diameter. Bake as for the straws. Allow to cool on the tray.
To serve, arrange bundles of the straws in the cheese rings. Garnish with parsley.

CHEESIES

$\frac{3}{4}$ cup self-raising flour
Pinch cayenne pepper
$\frac{1}{4}$ teaspoon salt
$\frac{3}{4}$ cup grated cheese
3 tablespoons melted butter
Coconut

Sift the flour into a bowl with the cayenne and salt then add the cheese. Pour in the melted butter, making a rather dry dough.
Take teaspoonsful and roll into balls, then roll each ball in coconut. Place on a greased shallow tray and press flat with the back of a fork. Bake in a slow oven, 160° C (325° F), for about 15 minutes or until the cheesies are a golden brown.

CHICKEN CANAPÉS

1 cup finely chopped cooked chicken
2 teaspoons mayonnaise
$\frac{1}{2}$ cup chopped salted almonds
2 tablespoons chopped sweet pickle
Cracker biscuits

Garnish: sliced stuffed olives

Blend the chicken with the mayonnaise. Stir in the almonds and pickle. Spread on small cracker biscuits and garnish with slices of stuffed olives.

CHICKEN CROUTES

12 small rounds fried bread *or* 12 small cracker biscuits
125 g (4 oz) chicken *or* ham, chopped finely
1 tablespoon mayonnaise
Small tomatoes
Salt and pepper

Garnish: 12 stuffed olives

Drain the rounds of fried bread, or butter the biscuits.
Mix finely chopped chicken or ham with the mayonnaise. Cut the tomatoes into 12 thin slices.
Place a slice of tomato on each croute or biscuit and season with salt and pepper. Add a little of the chicken mixture to each, and top with a stuffed olive.

CHILLED CHICKEN ROLLS

Brown bread
Butter, softened
1 cup chopped cooked chicken
1 tablespoon mayonnaise
Salt and pepper

Garnish: sprigs of parsley

Trim the crusts from thin slices of brown bread. Flatten each slice by rolling it with a rolling-pin on a damp cloth. Spread with softened butter.
Mix the chicken with about 1 tablespoon mayonnaise, and season to taste with salt and pepper. Spread on the bread. Tuck a sprig of parsley in at each end and roll up. Wrap in waxed paper and then in a damp cloth, and chill until serving time.

CURRIED CHICKEN BOATS

1 small can chicken and veal paste
2 teaspoons chutney
1 teaspoon curry powder
⅓ cup chopped toasted almonds
125 g (4 oz) jar of cream cheese spread
3 dozen pastry boats

Garnish: stuffed olives *or* gherkins

Blend the meat paste with the chutney, curry powder, almonds and cheese spread. Chill until just before serving. Spoon a little into each pastry boat and garnish with stuffed olives or gherkins.

DEVILLED ALMONDS

125 g (4 oz) almonds
45 g (1½ oz) butter *or*
   3 tablespoons olive oil
Salt
Cayenne pepper

Place the almonds in a saucepan, cover with cold water and bring to the boil. Remove from the heat, drain, remove the brown skins and dry the almonds.
Heat the butter or oil in a frying pan and, when very hot, add the almonds. Stir occasionally until they are lightly browned all over.
Lift out and drain on paper. Sprinkle with salt and cayenne, shaking the paper to make sure the seasonings cover the almonds.

DEVILLED HAM BITES

2 cups plain flour
¼ teaspoon cayenne pepper
125 g (4 oz) butter
1 can devilled ham paste
Butter, melted
Poppy seeds

Sift the flour with the cayenne and rub in the 4 ounces of butter until the mixture is crumbly. Stir in the ham paste, forming the mixture into a dough. Chill for about 30 minutes.
Roll out on a lightly floured board to about 5 mm (¼ in) thick and cut into 5 cm (2 in) rounds with a fluted cutter. Place on greased shallow oven trays. Brush the top of each round with melted butter and sprinkle with poppy seeds. Bake at 200° C (400° F) for 10 to 12 minutes. Remove from the oven and allow to cool on the trays.

DEVILLED HAM CORNUCOPIAS

20 slices bread
Butter, melted
Cocktail picks

Filling

2 teaspoons mayonnaise
1 small jar devilled ham
2 hard-boiled eggs, chopped finely
2 teaspoons prepared mustard
Paprika *or* parsley, chopped finely

Take 20 thin slices of bread and cut into rounds with a 5 cm (2 in) cutter. Flatten each round with a rolling-pin and spread both sides with melted butter. Roll up to form cornucopias (cones) and secure with cocktail picks. Place on a shallow oven tray and bake at 180° C (350° F) for 15 minutes or until lightly browned. Remove the picks.

Combine all filling ingredients except the last item. Chill the mixture, then fill each bread cornucopia with a generous teaspoonful. Sprinkle with paprika or finely chopped parsley.

HAM AND CHEESE BALLS

125 g (4 oz) cream cheese
185 g (6 oz) ham *or* corned beef, chopped finely
½ teaspoon Worcestershire sauce
2 teaspoons chopped pickle
Lemon juice
Pinch cayenne pepper
Salt
Chives, minced
Parsley, chopped finely

These may be prepared the day before they are required.
Soften the cream cheese and blend in thoroughly the very finely chopped ham or corned beef and the Worcestershire sauce, pickle, squeeze lemon juice, cayenne and salt (add salt sparingly). Take portions and form into balls about the size of a marble.
Just before serving, roll the balls in equal quantities of chives and parsley mixed together.

HAM AND CHEESE ROLLS

Straight bread rolls
2 tablespoons soft butter
125 g (4 oz) tasty cheese, grated
3 anchovies, chopped
185 g (6 oz) ham, chopped or minced
1 hard-boiled egg
1 tablespoon mayonnaise

Cut the ends off each straight bread roll and scoop out the bread, leaving a crust shell. Mix the butter, cheese, anchovies, ham, chopped hard-boiled egg and mayonnaise to make a stiff paste. Blend thoroughly and pack firmly into the breadroll crusts. Wrap in foil and chill for several hours. Cut each roll into 5–10 mm (¼–½ in) slices before serving.

PARTY SANDWICH LOAF

The fillings used are a matter of personal taste. Our loaf contains cheese and gherkin, chicken salad, ham salad and egg salad fillings.

Filling
CHEESE AND GHERKIN
185 g (6 oz) sharp flavoured cheese, grated
1½ tablespoons warm milk
1 tablespoon gherkin, chopped

CHICKEN SALAD
½ cup minced cooked chicken
½ cup finely chopped celery
1 tablespoon pickle *or* chutney
½ teaspoon salt
Pinch pepper
1 tablespoon mayonnaise

HAM SALAD
2 cups minced cooked ham *or* luncheon meat
1 tablespoon minced green pepper
½ teaspoon prepared mustard
2 teaspoons chopped shallot *or* onion
1 tablespoon mayonnaise

EGG SALAD
2 hard-boiled eggs, chopped
1 tablespoon finely chopped olives *or* gherkins
½ teaspoon salt
⅛ teaspoon pepper
½ teaspoon prepared mustard
1 tablespoon mayonnaise

Covering

3 125 g (4 oz) packets cream cheese
½ cup cream *or* top milk
1 sandwich loaf fresh *or* day-old bread

Garnish: radish roses, celery curls, cucumber slices

Topping: parsley, chopped finely

Cheese and gherkin filling. Mix grated sharp-flavoured cheese to a paste with warm milk and add gherkin.
Chicken salad filling. Combine and chill minced cooked chicken, finely chopped celery, pickle or chutney, salt, pepper and mayonnaise.
Ham salad filling. Combine and chill minced cooked ham or luncheon meat, minced green pepper, prepared mustard, chopped shallot or onion and mayonnaise.
Egg salad filling. Combine and chill chopped hard-boiled eggs, finely chopped olives or gherkins, salt, pepper, prepared mustard and mayonnaise.

To assemble the loaf

Blend the cream cheese with the cream to a good spreading consistency. Trim all the crusts from the bread and cut it lengthwise into five slices of even thickness.
Place one slice of bread on a board and cover evenly with the cheese and gherkin filling. Cover with the second slice of bread and add the chicken salad filling, spreading it evenly. Add the third slice of bread and top with the egg salad filling, then the fourth slice and the ham salad filling. Top with the remaining slice of bread. Press lightly but firmly together.
Spread the top, sides and ends evenly with cream cheese, then roughen it slightly to give a frosted appearance. Place on a serving dish, surround with the radish roses, celery curls and cucumber slices and sprinkle the top with the finely chopped parsley.

LIVERWURST CANAPÉS

180 g (6 oz) liverwurst
1 teaspoon tomato sauce
¼ teaspoon prepared horseradish
1 teaspoon prepared mustard
1 teaspoon Worcestershire sauce
10 slices pumpernickel
Butter

Garnish: stuffed olives, sliced

Remove the liverwurst from its casing and let it stand at room temperature to soften before mixing with the tomato sauce, horseradish, mustard and Worcestershire sauce. Stir until smooth. Spread on buttered rounds of pumpernickel and garnish with slices of stuffed olive.

SALMON SAVOURIES

125 g (4 oz) can of salmon
1½ tablespoons mayonnaise
1 tablespoon finely minced celery
¼ teaspoon Worcestershire sauce
¼ teaspoon chilli sauce
1 teaspoon lemon juice
Thin slices peeled cucumber
Butter
Thin slices white bread

Garnish: celery and parsley

Drain and flake the salmon and mix with the mayonnaise, celery, sauces and lemon juice.
Butter the bread and cover half the slices with the thinly sliced cucumber. Spread with the salmon mixture. Cover with the remaining buttered bread to make sandwiches. Press firmly and cut off the crusts. Wrap in greaseproof paper and chill for several hours.
To prepare for serving, cut each sandwich into three, then into two. Serve with a celery and parsley garnish.

ANCHOVY BISCUIT CREAMS

90 g (3 oz) plain flour
¼ teaspoon cayenne
45 g (1½ oz) butter
1 egg yolk
1 teaspoon anchovy essence
Good squeeze lemon juice
Cold water, as required

Topping

4 anchovies
1 hard-boiled egg
1 teaspoon soft butter
2 tablespoons cream, whipped

Garnish: parsley sprigs

Sift the flour and cayenne into a bowl and rub in the butter. Mix to a rather firm dough with the beaten egg yolk, anchovy essence and lemon juice plus a little cold water if the dough seems too dry. Turn on to a lightly floured board, knead lightly then roll thinly. Cut into rounds with a small cutter (about 4 cm or 1½ inches) and bake in a moderate oven for about 10 or 12 minutes. Cool.
Pound the anchovies with the butter and hard-boiled egg then press through a sieve. Whip the cream and beat into the mixture. Pipe a swirl of the anchovy cream on each cooled biscuit and garnish with tiny parsley sprigs.

PEANUT COCKTAIL BISCUITS

1 cup plain flour
½ level teaspoon salt
1 level teaspoon mustard
Pinch cayenne pepper
60 g (2 oz) butter
125 g (4 oz) cheese, grated
1 egg yolk
Cold water, as required
1 egg white
1 cup chopped salted peanuts

Sift the flour with the salt, mustard and cayenne. Rub in the butter and add the grated cheese. Mix to a rather dry dough with the egg yolk, adding a little water if necessary.
Turn on to a floured board and knead until smooth on the outside. Roll thinly and cut into rounds, using a 5 cm (2 in) cutter. Brush the tops with egg white and sprinkle with the chopped peanuts. Place on a shallow tray and bake in a hot oven, 220° C (425° F), for about 12 minutes.

OLIVE CHEESE BALL

250 g (½ lb) packaged cream cheese
250 g (½ lb) blue-vein cheese
125 g (4 oz) butter, soft
½ cup chopped green olives
1 tablespoon chopped shallots *or* chives
½ cup finely chopped walnuts
Cracker biscuits

Soften the cream cheese to room temperature, beat until creamy then beat in the crumbled blue-vein cheese and the soft butter. Add the olives and shallots or chives and chill until you can mould it into a ball. Chill again then roll in the chopped walnuts and serve with your favorite cracker biscuits.

Caviare Canapés 2 (p. 12).

Prune Savouries (p. 20).

HAZELNUT CHEESE BITES

125 g (4 oz) blue-vein cheese
¾ cup chopped toasted hazelnuts
Pinch salt
1 small can of pineapple pieces
Cocktail picks

Cream the cheese and stir in the nuts. Add the salt. Take portions and roll into small balls. Chill until firm.
Drain the pineapple pieces and place a hazelnut cheese-ball and a piece of pineapple on each cocktail pick. Spear them into an apple or an orange and serve on a platter.

SESAME BITES

5 tablespoons plain flour
½ teaspoon salt
Pinch cayenne pepper
¼ teaspoon dry mustard
60 g (2 oz) butter *or* margarine
60 g (2 oz) cheese, grated
Sesame seeds
1 egg yolk
½ teaspoon lemon juice
Milk for glazing

Sift the flour, salt, cayenne and mustard. Rub in the butter, then add the grated cheese and 1 tablespoon of sesame seeds.
Beat the egg yolk and the lemon juice together and add to the dry ingredients, making into a firm dough.
Knead lightly on a floured board and roll 5 mm (¼ in) thick. Cut into shapes with a small floured biscuit cutter. Brush the tops with a little milk and sprinkle with sesame seeds. Place on an ungreased shallow oven tray and bake in a moderate oven, 180° C (350° F), until a pale golden colour—about 12 to 15 minutes. Cool on the tray.

STUFFED EGGS

6 hard-boiled eggs
½ level teaspoon salt
¼ teaspoon cayenne pepper
½ level teaspoon dry mustard
½ teaspoon Worcestershire sauce
1½ tablespoons mayonnaise *or* salad dressing

Shell the eggs and cut in halves lengthwise. Remove the yolks and place in a bowl, keeping the whites intact. Mash the yolks or press them through a fine sieve. Mix in the salt, pepper, mustard, Worcestershire sauce and mayonnaise. Pipe or pile back into the egg-whites.

ZIPPY STUFFED EGGS

6 hard-boiled eggs
1 teaspoon gherkin spread
½ teaspoon Worcestershire sauce
1 teaspoon mustard sauce
Cream

Garnish: gherkin *or* olive, sliced

Shell the eggs and cut each in halves lengthwise. Scoop out the yolks without breaking the whites. Mash the yolks and mix them with the gherkin spread, Worcestershire sauce, mustard sauce and enough cream to make a spreading consistency.
Spoon the mixture into the egg-white cases and garnish each with a slice of gherkin or olive.

HOT SAVOURIES

Hot savouries are a truly delicious way to welcome your guests. They pleasantly complement the cold savouries you may prepare and, though many are very simple to make, give the effect of being rather "special" since many people these days do not want to go to the extra trouble they involve. In fact these welcome, piquant little titbits may often be prepared in less time than it takes to make cold hors d'œvres, especially if you use ready-made savoury boat or choux pastry cases.

APPETISER MEATBALLS WITH FLAVOURED SAUCES

Meatballs
750 g (1½ lbs) steak, minced finely
½ cup soft white breadcrumbs
2 tablespoons milk
1½ teaspoons salt
1 egg
1 clove garlic, crushed

Combine the minced steak, breadcrumbs, milk, salt, egg and crushed garlic, blending lightly. Shape into balls about the size of a large marble. Arrange on shallow trays and bake in a hot oven, 260° C (500° F), for about 5 minutes or until lightly browned. (Alternatively, fry them in a little oil or butter until brown all over.) Remove and add to the prepared sauce (recipes follow), including any pan drippings. Reheat the meatballs and serve with sauce.

STROGANOFF SAUCE

125 g (4 oz) butter *or* margarine
1 small onion, chopped
2 tablespoons plain flour
1½ cups beef broth
½ cup commercial sour cream
½ teaspoon dill
Salt and pepper
125 g (4 oz) can buttered mushrooms

Heat the butter in a pan and add chopped onion. Sauté until tender but not brown. Stir in the flour, cook until blended and bubbly. Slowly stir in the broth. Cook, stirring until thickened. Add the sour cream, dill, salt and pepper to taste, and the mushrooms. Reheat until boiling.

SWEET AND SOUR SAUCE

2 425 g (15 oz) cans pineapple pieces
1¼ cups chicken stock
¼ cup brown sugar
¾ cup vinegar
2 teaspoons soy sauce
2 teaspoons tomato sauce
3 rounded tablespoons cornflour
Cold stock or water
1 cup chopped spring onions
3 small green peppers, seeded and cut into cubes

Drain the syrup from the pineapple and combine it with the chicken stock, brown sugar, vinegar, and soy and tomato sauces. Blend the cornflour with a little cold stock or water and stir into the mixture. Cook, stirring well over medium heat until the sauce boils and thickens. Add the chopped onions and the cubed green peppers. Simmer for 5 minutes. Add the pineapple pieces. Reheat before serving.

ITALIAN TOMATO SAUCE

4 rashers bacon, diced
1 medium-sized onion, chopped finely
1 clove garlic, crushed
1 875 g (1 lb 15 oz) can tomatoes
1 teaspoon basil
1 teaspoon oregano
1 bayleaf
½ cup beef stock
1 tablespoon cornflour
¼ cup red wine *or* stock
1 teaspoon sugar
½ teaspoon salt
¼ teaspoon pepper

Dice the bacon and sauté until crisp. Drain from the pan (and discard) all but 1 tablespoon of the fat. Add finely chopped onion, crushed garlic and the tomatoes, basil, oregano, bayleaf and stock.
Bring to the boil and simmer for 30 minutes. Blend together the cornflour, red wine or stock, sugar, salt and pepper. Stir into the tomato mixture and cook, stirring well, until the mixture boils and thickens. Reheat the meatballs and serve with the sauce.

CURRY SAUCE

¼ cup butter
1 large onion, chopped finely
1 clove garlic crushed
1 level tablespoon curry powder
2 tablespoons plain flour
2 teaspoons sugar
½ teaspoon salt
Pinch cayenne pepper
1½ cups chicken stock or water with 1 chicken-soup cube
½ cup cream

Heat the butter in a large saucepan. Sauté finely chopped onion until soft but not brown. Add crushed garlic, then curry powder, and cook for 1 minute. Add the flour, sugar, salt and cayenne and cook until smooth. Stir in the stock and the cream. Cook, stirring well until the mixture boils and thickens. Simmer for 3 minutes. Reheat the meatballs and serve with the sauce.

SWEDISH MEATBALLS

375 g (¾ lb) steak, minced finely
¾ cup dry breadcrumbs
¾ teaspoon cornflour
1 small onion, peeled and minced
Pinch allspice
1 egg, beaten
½ cup cream
½ teaspoon salt
1 clove garlic, crushed
Cocktail picks

Combine all the ingredients in a bowl and mix well. Shape into small balls in a little seasoned flour.
Heat about 2 tablespoons of fat or oil in a frying pan and cook the meatballs until they are golden on all sides and cooked through. This will take about 12 minutes. Drain well.
For a party savoury these meatballs may be made the day before they are required, then covered with foil and reheated in a moderated oven. Stick a cocktail pick into each meatball and serve as a savoury.

FISH BALLS

2 cups dry mashed potato
1 198 g (7 oz) can of herrings in tomato sauce
1 teaspoon tarragon vinegar
1 egg
2 tablespoons milk
1 cup breadcrumbs
Seasoned flour, as needed
Oil *or* fat for frying

Place the mashed potato in a bowl. Mash the herrings and mix them with the potato. Flavour with the tarragon vinegar and bind with a little beaten egg. Beat the remaining egg into the milk.
Take teaspoonsful of the fish mixture and shape into small balls, using a little seasoned flour if necessary. Dip each ball in the egg glazing and then cover with breadcrumbs. Deep-fry in hot oil or fat until a golden brown. Drain on paper and serve as appetisers.

BACON SNACKS

Bacon
Prepared mustard
Skewers
Cocktail picks

Remove the rind from rashers of bacon. Spread the rashers with prepared mustard, roll them up and thread on skewers. Grill or bake until the bacon fat is clear. Serve hot on cocktail picks.

PRUNE SAVOURIES

Prunes
Rum
Pâté
Bacon
Cocktail picks

Remove the stones and soak the prunes overnight in rum. Drain, then fill each prune with a little pâté. Roll the prune in a piece of bacon and spear each with a cocktail pick. Place on a shallow tray and cook in a hot oven for about 10 minutes or until the bacon fat is clear. Serve hot.

PINEAPPLE AND BACON SAVOURIES

1 can pineapple pieces
Kirsch
Bacon
Cocktail picks

Drain the syrup from a can of pineapple pieces. Sprinkle the pieces with a little Kirsch and wrap individually in pieces of bacon. Spear each with a cocktail pick and place on a shallow tray. Cook in a hot oven for about 10 minutes or until the bacon fat is clear. Serve hot.

CRABMEAT BACON ROLLS

1 170 g (6 oz) can crabmeat
1 tablespoon tomato juice
Beaten egg
1 cup soft white breadcrumbs
Salt and pepper
1 teaspoon chopped parsley
1 teaspoon chopped celery leaves
12 bacon slices
Cocktail picks

Drain and flake the crabmeat, if necessary. Mix the tomato juice with the egg and add the breadcrumbs, seasonings, parsley, celery leaves and crabmeat. Mix thoroughly. Take small spoonsful and make into rolls about 5 cm (2 in) long.
Remove the rind from the bacon slices and cut them into pieces to wrap round the crabmeat rolls. Secure each with a cocktail pick. Place on a shallow oven tray and bake in a moderate oven for about 12 minutes, or until the bacon is cooked.

TITBITS

Take small strips of bacon and roll them round small pieces of cheese, chunks of pineapple, slices of cooked sausage or pieces of gherkin. Secure each with a cocktail pick. Place on a shallow baking tray. Bake or grill until the bacon is cooked. Serve hot.
For a cold savoury, use ham instead of bacon and do not cook.
Another way with bacon rolls is to remove the rind from streaky bacon rashers, cut each rasher into 2 or 3 pieces, and spread lightly with mustard or chutney, then roll the bacon round a chunky piece of banana, a stuffed olive, a cooked and peeled prawn or a sweet gherkin. Secure each with a cocktail pick and bake or grill until the bacon is cooked. Serve hot.

OYSTER AND BACON CANAPÉS

White bread rounds
Butter
Oysters, fresh or canned
Bacon

Lightly toast some rounds of white bread, then butter them. Place a fresh or canned oyster on each, then top the oyster with a small piece of bacon. Arrange the canapés on a flat oven tray and grill or bake until the bacon fat is clear. Serve hot.

TONGUE AND CHUTNEY CANAPÉS

½ cup finely chopped cooked tongue
½ cup chutney, chopped
¼ teaspoon cayenne pepper
½ teaspoon curry powder
20 rounds white bread, 4 cm (1½ in) in diameter
Mayonnaise
Cheese, grated

Mix together the tongue, chutney, cayenne and curry powder. Place the rounds of bread on a baking tray and cover them generously with the meat mixture. Dot with mayonnaise and sprinkle with grated cheese. Place in a hot oven, about 260° C (500° F), and bake for 5 minutes.

SAVOURY PINWHEELS

60 g (2 oz) butter
½ cup grated sharp cheese
2 teaspoons chopped parsley
1 teaspoon prepared mustard
2 teaspoons tomato sauce
1 teaspoon Worcestershire sauce
6 slices fresh bread about 3 mm (⅛ in) thick
Stuffed olives
Cocktail picks

Cream the butter and cheese, then blend in the next four ingredients.
Remove the crusts from the slices of bread and spread generously with the cheese mixture. Place a row of stuffed olives at one end. Roll each slice up like a jelly roll and fasten with cocktail picks. Wrap in greased paper and chill thoroughly.
Just before serving, cut each roll in two and toast until brown. Serve hot.
To serve cold, cut into slices 5 mm (¼ in) thick.

DEVILLED ALMOND CROUTES

60 g (2 oz) almonds, blanched and shredded
1 teaspoon oil
2 gherkins
1 chilli
Salt
Cayenne pepper
Fried bread rounds about 4 cm (1½ in) in diameter

Garnish: gherkin and chilli strips, parsley sprigs

Fry the almonds lightly in the oil. Cut some of the gherkins into strips as well as a little of the chilli. Chop the remainder and mix with the almonds. Season with salt and cayenne. Mix well and pile small spoonsful on the fried bread rounds. Decorate with the strips of gherkin and chilli and tiny parsley sprigs.

DEVILLED HAM CANAPÉS

1 can devilled ham
2 teaspoons mayonnaise
2 hard-boiled eggs, chopped
2 teaspoons prepared mustard
20 rounds of fried bread, each about 5 cm (2 in) in diameter
Parsley, chopped finely, *or* paprika

Combine the devilled ham with the mayonnaise, chopped eggs and mustard, blending well. Spread thickly on the rounds of fried bread. Sprinkle with parsley or paprika and serve hot or cold.

SMOKED HAM CANAPÉS

30 g (1 oz) butter
¼ cup boiling water
¼ cup sifted plain flour
¼ teaspoon salt
1 egg
¼ cup Swiss cheese, grated

Filling

125 g (4 oz) smoked ham sausage, chopped
⅓ cup finely chopped celery
1 tablespoon chopped green pepper
½ teaspoon prepared horseradish
⅓ cup mayonnaise or salad dressing

Melt the butter in the boiling water, then stir in the flour and the salt. Cook, stirring well over medium heat, until the mixture forms a ball which does not separate. Remove from the heat and cool slightly. Add the egg and beat vigorously until smooth. Stir in the cheese.
Take level teaspoonsful of the dough and drop on to a greased oven tray. Bake at 200° C (400° F) for 20 minutes. Remove from the tray and allow to cool.
To make the filling combine the chopped ham sausage with the remaining ingredients and chill. Just before serving split the puffs and fill them. Heat before serving.

HAM AND CHEESE TOASTIES

½ cup chopped ham
2 tablespoons chutney
Rounds or fingers toasted bread
Cream
1 or 2 tablespoons grated cheese

Blend the chopped ham and chutney and spread on the toasted bread. Moisten the surface of each with a little cream and sprinkle with the grated cheese. Heat in the oven until the cheese melts.

CANAPÉS MONTE CRISTO

Bread, small rounds
Ham, minced
Mustard
Cayenne pepper
Nutmeg
Salt
Mayonnaise
Cheddar cheese
Paprika

Toast small rounds of bread on one side and spread the untoasted side with butter. Top with minced ham flavoured with mustard, cayenne pepper, nutmeg and salt, and mixed to a spreading consistency with mayonnaise. Add a slice of Cheddar cheese (cut to the shape of the bread) and place on a baking tray. Dust the tops with paprika. Cook under a heated griller or in the top of a hot oven until the cheese melts and browns. Serve hot.

CHEESE MATCHSTICKS

White bread, preferably several days old
Melted butter
Cheese, grated
Cayenne pepper
Mustard

Slice the bread about 5 mm ($\frac{1}{4}$ in) thick and remove the crusts. Cut the slices into sticks about 8 cm (3 in) long (or the width of the sandwich loaf) and $\frac{1}{4}$ inch wide and dip into melted butter.
Mix some grated cheese with a little cayenne and mustard and toss the bread in the mixture, making sure each piece is thoroughly coated.
Place on a baking tray and bake in a moderate oven, 170° C (350° F), until the sticks become crisp and lightly brown. They may be served hot or cold, but are best when hot.

CHEESE PUFFS

1 cup self-raising flour
$\frac{1}{2}$ teaspoon salt
Pinch cayenne pepper
30 g (1 oz) butter
$\frac{3}{4}$ cup grated Cheddar cheese
1 egg, beaten
2 to 3 tablespoons milk
Hot oil *or* lard for frying

Sift the flour, salt and cayenne. Rub in the butter and add all but 2 tablespoons of the grated cheese. Mix into a scone dough with the combined beaten egg and milk. Turn on to a lightly floured board and knead until smooth.
Form the dough into a long roll about 2.5 cm (1 in) in diameter. Cut off pieces about 1 cm ($\frac{1}{2}$ in) thick and roll into balls. Drop them into deep hot oil or lard and fry for 3 to 4 minutes. Drain on paper. Toss them in the reserved cheese. Serve hot.

PINEAPPLE AND HAM PUFFS

125 g (4 oz) self-raising flour
$\frac{1}{4}$ teaspoon salt
$\frac{1}{4}$ teaspoon cayenne pepper
30 g (1 oz) butter
$\frac{1}{2}$ cup chopped cooked ham
$\frac{1}{2}$ cup diced, well drained pineapple
1 egg
2 teaspoons milk
1 tablespoon mayonnaise
Hot oil *or* fat
Cocktail picks

Sift the flour, salt and cayenne into a bowl. Rub in the butter and add the ham and pineapple. Beat the egg with the milk and mayonnaise and add to the mixture making a light, soft dough. Take teaspoonsful of the mixture and drop into deep, hot oil or fat. Fry until a golden brown. Drain on paper and serve hot on cocktail picks.

CURRIED TUNA PUFFS

Choux Pastry

$\frac{2}{3}$ cup cold water
30 g (1 oz) butter
60 g (2 oz) plain flour
2 eggs

Filling

1 onion, peeled and minced
1 tomato, chopped
1 tablespoon butter
1$\frac{1}{4}$ cups milk
1 213 g (7 oz) can tuna
2 teaspoons curry powder
3 tablespoons plain flour
Salt and pepper
Lemon juice

Place the water and butter for the pastry in a saucepan and bring to the boil. Remove from the heat, add the sifted flour and stir until smooth. Return the saucepan to the heat and cook, stirring constantly until the mixture leaves the sides of the saucepan. Turn into a bowl and allow to cool.
Beat the eggs until twice their original size and add gradually to the flour mixture. The resulting mixture should be smooth and shiny.
Place teaspoonsful on to a shallow, greased tray and bake in a moderate oven for 20 to 25 minutes. Cool.
Melt the butter for the filling in a saucepan, add the minced onion and cook until it is soft but not brown. Add the tomato and cook until soft. Stir in the flour and curry powder and cook for a further two or three minutes then add the milk and cook, stirring constantly until the sauce boils and thickens. Add the drained tuna and season to taste with salt, pepper and lemon juice.
Place a spoonful in each cooked choux pastry case and reheat in a moderate oven for about 10 minutes. Serve hot.

SAVOURY BOATS

2 cups plain flour
$\frac{1}{2}$ level teaspoon baking powder
Pinch salt
125 g (4 oz) butter *or* margarine
2 tablespoons water with a squeeze lemon juice

Sift the flour with the baking powder and salt. Rub in the butter and mix to a firm dough with the water and lemon juice. Turn on to a lightly floured board and knead only until smooth on the outside.

Roll thinly and cut into shapes to line patty tins or boat-shaped tins. Prick the bottom of each to prevent the centre rising. Bake in a hot oven, 200° C (400° F), for 12 to 15 minutes or until lightly browned. Remove from the tins and allow to cool.

CURRIED CHICKEN FILLING

½ cup diced peeled apple
¼ cup chopped onion
1 clove garlic, crushed
1 tablespoon butter
1 tablespoon plain flour
Salt and pepper
1 teaspoon curry powder
1 cup chicken stock
1½ cups diced cooked chicken
1 teaspoon chopped parsley

Sauté the apple, onion and garlic in the butter for 5 minutes without browning. Stir in the flour with salt and pepper to taste and the curry powder. Stir until smooth, then cook for 1 minute. Add the chicken stock and cook, stirring well, until the mixture boils and thickens. Add the diced chicken and cook until thoroughly heated. Use to fill the cooked pastry shells. Sprinkle with chopped parsley. This quantity will fill about 2 dozen boats.

BRAIN AND WALNUT FILLING

1 set brains, cooked
1¼ cups white sauce
1 rounded tablespoon chopped walnuts
1 teaspoon chopped parsley
Salt
Cayenne pepper

Garnish: parsley sprigs *or* stuffed olives

Cut the brains into small pieces and mix into the sauce with the walnuts and parsley. Season with salt and cayenne pepper. Place a spoonful in each pastry boat and reheat before serving. Garnish with sprigs of parsley (or stuffed olives).

OYSTER PATTIES

250 g (½ lb) puff pastry
30 g (1 oz) butter
2 level tablespoons plain flour
Salt
Pinch cayenne pepper
¼ teaspoon mustard (optional)
½ cup milk
3 tablespoons oyster liquid
1½ dozen oysters
1 tablespoon cream
1 teaspoon anchovy sauce (optional)

Garnish: lemon and parsley

Roll the pastry 5 mm (¼ in) thick. Using a 4 cm (1½ in) round cutter, cut into rounds. With a 1 cm (½ in) cutter mark the centre of each round and cut halfway through. (If the cutters are dipped in almost boiling water each time they are used, the cut will be cleaner and the pastry will rise better.) Place on a shallow oven tray and bake in a hot oven, 230° C (450° F) for about 10 to 12 minutes.

To make the filling, melt the butter in a small saucepan and add the flour, salt, cayenne and mustard. Stir until smooth and cook for 1 minute without browning. Add the milk and oyster liquid and stir until the sauce boils and thickens. Cook for 2 minutes. Add the bearded oysters, cream and anchovy sauce (if you have included the mustard omit anchovy sauce).

Remove the tops from the baked cases, add a teaspoonful of the cream oyster mixture to each, and replace its top. Reheat if necessary. Serve hot, garnished with lemon and parsley.

PARTY PIES

Potato pastry

1 cup plain flour
1 level teaspoon baking powder
¼ teaspoon salt
60 g (2 oz) butter
1½ cups dry mashed potato
1 egg

Fillings

MUSHROOM
2 teaspoons butter
1 small onion, chopped
1 250 g (8 oz) can sliced mushrooms
Salt and pepper
1½ teaspoons cream *or* top milk

CURRY
1 small onion, chopped finely
2 teaspoons butter
½ cup chopped cooked ham *or* beef
½ small tomato, chopped
1 cup cold cooked rice
Pinch salt
1 teaspoon curry powder

Sift the flour, baking powder and salt into a bowl and rub in the butter. Add the mashed potato and mix to a smooth dough with the well-beaten egg. Cover and chill for about 1 hour.

Place the pastry on a lightly floured board and roll to about 3 mm (⅛ in) thick. Cut into rounds with a floured pastry cutter and use to line greased patty tins. Add a teaspoonful of the desired filling, then top with another round of potato pastry. Brush the tops with beaten egg and milk. Bake at 230° C (450° F) for 10 to 15 minutes. Serve hot.

Mushroom filling. Melt butter in a pan and sauté onion until soft but not brown. Add mushrooms, salt and pepper to taste, and cream or top milk. Mix well and allow to cool before using.

Curry filling. Sauté onion in butter until soft but not brown. Add ham or beef, tomato, rice, salt and curry powder.

SWISS ONION CAKE

1½ cups plain flour
1 teaspoon sugar
½ teaspoon salt
125 g (4 oz) butter *or* margarine
3 tablespoons milk

Filling

4 slices bacon
2 medium-sized onions
2 eggs, beaten
1 egg yolk, beaten
¾ cup sour or fresh cream
1 tablespoon plain flour
½ teaspoon salt
Pepper

Sift the flour, sugar and salt into a bowl. Rub in the
butter and mix to a light dough with the milk. Pat
two-thirds of the dough into the bottom of a
greased 8 in sandwich tin. Bake at 220° C (425° F)
for about 10 minutes or until lightly browned. Cool.
Reduce the oven temperature to 160° C (325° F).
Cut the bacon into 5 mm (¼ in) strips and fry until
crisp. Drain, remove from the pan. Chop the onions
and cook in the bacon fat until tender. Combine the
remaining ingredients with the bacon and onion.
Pat the left-over one-third of the dough round the
edge of the cooled, cooked pastry mixture, pour in
the filling and bake until set, about 20 minutes. Cut
into wedges and serve.

DIPS SPREADS & PATÉS

Dips are popular at every party, and here you will find many delicious suggestions. Serve your dips accompanied by cracker biscuits, crisp celery sticks, carrot sticks, cauliflower flowerets, radish roses, potato crisps or miniature fingers of Melba toast.

Pâté, one of the famous dishes we have adopted from the French cuisine, is fast becoming a favourite—especially as a first course appetiser. If you haven't a blender for puréeing the mixture, pass the meats twice through your mincer, using the finest blade, or pound with a pestle in a mortar. Smoothness is the essence of success in this dish.

AVOCADO AND TUNA DIP

1 medium-sized avocado
125 g (4 oz) drained tuna
1 tablespoon chopped parsley
1 teaspoon chopped chives
2 drops Worcestershire sauce
$\frac{1}{4}$ teaspoon mustard
1 teaspoon mayonnaise
Salt and pepper

Halve the avocado and scoop out the flesh. Place it in a bowl with the other ingredients and beat to a smooth consistency. Use as a dip or make a little firmer and spread on cracker biscuits.

AVOCADO BUTTER

1 medium-sized avocado
185 g (6 oz) soft butter
1½ teaspoons gelatine
1 tablespoon boiling water
1 tablespoon cream
1 tablespoon lemon juice
Pinch garlic salt (optional)

Peel and mash the avocado, add the softened butter and beat until thoroughly blended.
Soften the gelatine in the boiling water and stir until it dissolves. Cool slightly and add the cream. Add this mixture to the avocado together with the lemon juice, and the garlic salt if liked. Turn into a small dish and spread, smoothing the top. Cover and chill thoroughly. (It will keep in the refrigerator for about a week, or it can be frozen and kept longer.)

GUACAMOLE

2 ripe avocados
2 teaspoons lemon juice
2 teaspoons white onion *or* shallot, chopped finely
1 teaspoon salt
$\frac{1}{4}$ teaspoon chilli powder
$\frac{1}{3}$ cup mayonnaise
4 slices bacon, chopped and crisply cooked

Peel and mash the avocados (you should have about two cups). Place in a bowl and add the lemon juice, onion, salt and chilli powder. Mix well.
Spread the mayonnaise on the surface of the mixture making sure it reaches the edges to completely seal in the flavors. Chill for several hours or overnight. At serving time stir in the layer of mayonnaise, add the bacon and mix well.
Serve as a dip with crackers or corn chips.

CREAMY CHIVE DIP

125 g (4 oz) packet cream cheese
1 tablespoon mayonnaise
1 or 2 tablespoons milk
1 teaspoon chopped parsley
$\frac{1}{2}$ teaspoon Worcestershire sauce
1 tablespoon chopped chives
1 teaspoon mixed mustard
1 or 2 hard-boiled eggs

Allow the cream cheese to soften to room temperature. Beat until soft and fluffy, then mix in the mayonnaise, 1 tablespoon milk, the parsley, Worcestershire sauce, chives and mustard. Add the chopped eggs and enough milk to make a dip consistency.

OLIVE DIP

125 g (4 oz) cream cheese
1 tablespoon milk
Pinch curry powder
$\frac{1}{4}$ teaspoon finely chopped onion
$\frac{1}{2}$ cup chopped olives
Pinch paprika

Place the cream cheese and the milk in a bowl and cream well. Add the remaining ingredients and blend well. Chill before using.

CREAMY SPRING ONION DIP

125 g (4 oz) cream cheese
1 tablespoon cream
1 teaspoon sherry
1 tablespoon spring onion, chopped

Place the cream cheese and the cream in a bowl and blend. Add remaining ingredients and mix well. Chill before using.

PINEAPPLE DIP

125 g (4 oz) cream cheese
1 tablespoon canned unsweetened milk *or* cream
Salt and pepper
2 tablespoons crushed pineapple
1 or 2 tablespoons finely diced cooked bacon

Place the cream cheese and the milk in a bowl and cream well. Add the remaining ingredients and blend well. Chill before using.

BLUE CHEESE DIP

180 g (6 oz) cream cheese
3 tablespoons milk
125 g (4 oz) blue-vein cheese, crumbled
1 tablespoon finely chopped spring onion
$\frac{1}{2}$ cup chopped olives
Salt and pepper

Beat the cream cheese until light. Gradually beat in the milk, then add the blue-vein cheese, spring onion and olives, with salt and pepper to taste. Blend well. Chill before using.

CHOPPED ALMOND SPREAD

$1\frac{1}{2}$ tablespoons finely chopped toasted almonds
125 g (4 oz) cream cheese
2 teaspoons chutney, chopped
Pinch salt
Cream
Cracker biscuits *or* Melba toast

Blend the almonds with the cream cheese, chutney, salt and enough cream to make the mixture spread easily.
Spread generously on cracker biscuits or Melba toast.

CHICKEN AND ALMOND DIP

$\frac{1}{2}$ cup finely chopped cooked chicken
1 tablespoon chopped celery
1 tablespoon chopped browned almonds
1 tablespoon chopped parsley
Mayonnaise

Combine the chicken, celery, almonds and parsley. Mix well, then add enough mayonnaise to make a dip or spread consistency.

CHICKEN LIVER AND MUSHROOM DIP

250 g (½ lb) chicken livers
4 level tablespoons butter
1 small can mushrooms
2 tablespoons very finely chopped onion
¼ cup finely chopped parsley
Salt and pepper to taste
½ cup mayonnaise

Sauté the chicken livers in the butter until brown. Place on the chopping board and chop, or put through the mincer. Place in a bowl with the remaining ingredients, adding enough mayonnaise to make a dip consistency.

CRUNCHY HAM DIP

1 cup sour *or* fresh cream
1 cup chopped cooked ham
½ cup chopped blanched almonds or peanuts
2 teaspoons Worcestershire sauce
2 teaspoons prepared mustard
Pinch cayenne pepper

If using fresh cream, whip until it begins to thicken. Combine the cream with the other ingredients and beat until well mixed. Chill for 2 to 3 hours.

EGG AND PARSLEY DIP

125 g (4 oz) cream cheese
Pinch each salt and pepper
Pinch mixed herbs
1 tablespoon lemon juice
2 teaspoons finely chopped onion
½ teaspoon Worcestershire sauce
½ teaspoon mixed mustard
Mayonnaise *or* cream
3 hard-boiled eggs, chopped
2 teaspoons finely chopped parsley

Beat the cream cheese until smooth. Add the salt, pepper, herbs, lemon juice, onion, Worcestershire sauce and mustard, blending thoroughly. Add enough mayonnaise or cream to make a dip consistency. Fold in the chopped eggs and the parsley.

DEVILLED EGG AND TUNA DIP

3 hard-boiled eggs, mashed
1 teaspoon anchovy paste
½ small can tuna, drained and flaked
1 teaspoon finely minced onion
Garlic salt to taste
Pinch cayenne pepper
Dash Tabasco sauce
Mayonnaise

Combine all the ingredients, using just enough mayonnaise to make a dip consistency.

CRAB DIP

250 g (½ lb) packaged cream cheese
¼ cup cream
2 teaspoons lemon juice
1½ teaspoons Worcestershire sauce
1 clove garlic, peeled and crushed
¼ teaspoon salt
Pinch cayenne pepper
1 170 g (5½ oz) can crab meat, well drained

Have the cream cheese softened to room temperature then beat it until smooth, gradually adding the cream. Flavour with the lemon juice, sauce, garlic, salt and cayenne. After draining the crab remove any small bony bits and cut or chop into small pieces. Stir into the cheese mixture.
Chill before serving. Makes about 1¾ cups of dip.

ANCHOVY DIP

125 g (4 oz) packaged cream cheese
2 teaspoons anchovy paste
2 teaspoons onion, grated
3–4 drops lemon juice

Beat all ingredients together until smooth.

PRAWN DIP

175 g (5 oz) shelled prawns, chopped
250 g (½ lb) cream cheese
2 teaspoons Worcestershire sauce
½ teaspoon onion salt
Pinch cayenne pepper
Milk

Combine prawns with the cream cheese and the seasonings, adding enough milk to make a dip consistency.

CHIVE AND OYSTER DIP

125 g (4 oz) cream cheese
1 tablespoon mayonnaise
½ teaspoon Worcestershire sauce
½ teaspoon prepared mustard
3–4 drops lemon juice
2 teaspoons chopped chives
Salt and pepper
Cream *or* top milk
½ can smoked oysters, drained and chopped

Soften the cream cheese to room temperature and cream it until smooth. Add the mayonnaise, Worcestershire sauce, mustard, lemon juice and chives, seasoning to taste with salt and pepper. Blend thoroughly, adding a little cream or top milk to make a good dip consistency.

Chop the well-drained oysters and fold into the mixture. Chill well before using.

SMOKED OYSTER DIP

1 can smoked oysters, drained and finely chopped
125 g (4 oz) packet cream cheese
1 spring onion, chopped very finely
1 tablespoon very finely chopped celery
¼ teaspoon Worcestershire sauce
1 teaspoon lemon juice
Pepper and salt to taste
Pinch paprika
½ level teaspoon mustard
Milk

Combine all the ingredients except the milk in a bowl and beat until well blended. Add enough milk to make a smooth consistency (it should take only about a tablespoonful).

SMOKED OYSTER SPREAD

125 g (4 oz) cream cheese
1 small can smoked oysters, drained and chopped finely
2 teaspoons lemon juice
⅛ teaspoon chilli sauce

Soften the cream cheese and blend in the oysters. Season with the lemon juice and chilli sauce. Spread on small rounds of brown rye or pumpernickel bread or on cracker biscuits.

CREAMY CAVIARE DIP

125 g (4 oz) packaged cream cheese
1 cup cultivated sour cream
1 teaspoon finely chopped white onion
1 60 g (2 oz) jar caviare
Melba toast

Soften the cream cheese to room temperature then beat until smooth with the sour cream. Add the onion. Now very gently stir in the caviar. Serve in a bowl surrounded with the triangles of Melba toast.

CHICKEN LIVER PÂTÉ

125 g (4 oz) pork fillet, chopped
2 rashers rindless bacon, chopped
250 g (½ lb) chicken livers, washed and cleaned
1 clove garlic, crushed
4 shallots, chopped
1 large egg, chopped
1 tablespoon cornflour
2 tablespoons dry white wine
2 tablespoons Cointreau
¼ teaspoon salt
¼ teaspoon black pepper, freshly ground
¼ teaspoon nutmeg, grated
1 bay leaf
Toast triangles *or* cracker biscuits

Place pork and bacon both in the blender with the chicken livers, garlic and shallots. Blend until the mixture is a smooth paste. Add the egg, cornflour, white wine, Cointreau, salt, pepper and nutmeg. Blend again until thoroughly mixed.

Place a bay leaf in the bottom of a lightly greased two and a half cup capacity mould, or terrine, and spoon in the mixture. Cover with foil. Stand the mould in a dish containing enough cold water to come half way up the sides. Cook in a slow to moderate oven, 150° to 160° C (300° to 350° F) for about one hour.

Remove from the oven, place a weight on top and allow to cool. Unmould and serve with toast triangles or cracker biscuits.

PÂTÉ MAISON

125 g (4 oz) bacon, sliced thinly
3 tablespoons brandy
500 g (1 lb) lamb's liver
375 g (¾ lb) chicken livers
1 egg
2 tablespoons cream
1 teaspoon lemon juice
1 clove garlic, crushed
Salt and black pepper, freshly ground

Remove the rind and chop the bacon up roughly. Remove the skin and the white tubes from the lamb's liver and chop it roughly. Reserve 125 g (¼ lb) of the chicken liver and place the remainder with the bacon and lamb's liver in a blender. Blend until smooth. Add the egg, cream, lemon juice, garlic, salt and pepper to taste and blend again.

Heat the brandy, ignite it and pour over the liver mixture mixing with a fork.

Half fill a greased pate mould with some of this mixture, coarsely chop the reserved chicken livers and spread on top then cover with the remainder of the liver. Cover with foil.

Stand the mould in a pan of water and cook in a moderate oven for two hours. Remove from the heat and allow to cool. Now place a weight on top and press down firmly. Chill overnight and unmould before serving.

SPEEDY PÂTÉ

1 125 g (4 oz) can liverwurst
¼ teaspoon allspice
1 tablespoon cream
2 teaspoons brandy
Cracker biscuits

Empty the liverwurst into a small bowl and using a wooden spoon gradually beat in the remaining ingredients. Serve in a bowl accompanied by cracker biscuits.

PRAWN PÂTÉ

250 g (½ lb) cooked prawns
45 g (1½ oz) butter
60 g (2 oz) cream cheese
1 tablespoon mayonnaise
2 drops Tabasco sauce
1 small clove garlic, peeled and crushed
1 teaspoon lemon juice
1 tablespoon cream
French bread

Shell the prawns and chop them up very finely. In a small bowl beat the butter until creamy then beat in the cream cheese. Flavour to taste with the mayonnaise, Tabasco, garlic and lemon juice before beating in the chopped prawns. Add the cream and beat to blend.
Pack into a mould, cover with foil and refrigerate overnight if possible, or for a minimum of about five hours. Serve with slices of buttered French bread.

SALMON PÂTÉ

250 g (8 oz) cream cheese
2 teaspoons chilli sauce
1 tablespoon chopped parsley
1 tablespoon chopped shallot
½ teaspoon Tabasco sauce
500 g (1 lb) canned salmon
½ teaspoon salt
¼ teaspoon pepper
1 teaspoon lemon juice
Toast fingers or cracker biscuits

Garnish: stuffed olives, sliced

Place the cream cheese in a bowl and blend until smooth. Add the chilli sauce, parsley, shallot and Tabasco. Drain, bone and flake the salmon and blend smoothly into the mixture. Flavour with salt, pepper and lemon juice. Pack the mixture into a lightly oiled three cup capacity mould. Cover with foil and refrigerate for at least three hours.
Turn into a serving dish and garnish the top with slices of stuffed olives. Serve with toast fingers or cracker biscuits.

CHICKEN TERRINE

1.5 to 2 kg (3 to 4 lb) chicken breasts
1 bouquet garni (1 bay leaf, 1 stalk parsley, 1 sprig thyme)
1 carrot, chopped
2 stalks celery, chopped
375 g (12 oz) belly pork, chopped
2 onions, chopped
2 cloves garlic, peeled and crushed
1 tablespoon parsley, chopped
1 egg
1 small lemon, grated rind and juice
Salt and pepper
1 tablespoon gelatine
Toast triangles or tossed salad

Remove all the flesh from the chicken breasts. Place the bones in a saucepan with about two cups of cold water, some salt, a bouquet garni, pieces of carrot and celery. Cover and simmer for about one hour. This makes the stock which is used later for the jelly covering the terrine.
Take one third of the breast meat and cut it into strips. Place on one side. Chop the remainder and place in the blender with the pork, the onion, garlic and parsley. Blend until smooth. Now add the egg, lemon rind and juice and blend again. Season with salt and pepper. Place half this mixture in the bottom of a well greased terrine, lay the strips of chicken on top then cover with the remainder of the chicken and pork mixture. Cover with foil.
Stand terrine in a dish containing about 2.5 cm (1 in) water and cook in a moderate oven for about two and a half hours. Remove from the oven, place a weight on top and allow to cool.
Unmould. Wash the terrine pan and lightly oil it. Strain the stock you made with the chicken bones, add one tablespoon of gelatine and stir over heat until it has dissolved. Pour about 1 cm (½ in) into the terrine then replace the cooked meat. Fill with more jellied stock. Chill until firm. Unmould and serve either with toast triangles or a tossed salad.

CHICKEN LIVER TERRINE

500 g (1 lb) chicken livers, washed and cleaned
3 tablespoons port
¼ teaspoon thyme
3 or 4 bay leaves, crumbled
125 g (4 oz) cooked ham, chopped roughly
375 g (¾ lb) sausage meat
3 slices bread
Milk
4 tablespoons dry white wine
1 small clove garlic, peeled and crushed
Salt and black pepper, freshly ground
6 thin slices bacon, rind removed
Melted butter or lard
Cracker biscuits or toast triangles

Place the chicken livers in a bowl; add the port,

thyme and bay leaves. Marinate the mixture for at
least two hours. Take 375 g ($\frac{3}{4}$ lb) of the chicken
livers and place in the blender with the sausage
meat, ham and the bread which has been soaked in
milk. Blend until a paste consistency, then add the
white wine, garlic, and salt and pepper to taste.
Blend again. Place the bacon rashers between waxed
or greaseproof paper and beat until they are paper
thin. Use the rashers to line a pâté mould reserving
a few strips for the top. Spread half the chicken
liver mixture in the bottom of the mould, add the
whole chicken livers then cover with the remaining
mixture. Top with the reserved bacon rashers and
add a few bay leaves. Cover with foil. Stand the
mould in a dish containing boiling water. Cook in
a moderate oven for about 1$\frac{1}{2}$ hours. Remove from
the heat, place a weight on top to squeeze out excess
juices and allow to cool.

When the pâté is quite cold coat the surface with
melted butter or lard and refrigerate for two or
three days before serving.

To serve, unmould on to a platter and accompany
with cracker biscuits or toast triangles.

RABBIT TERRINE

500 g (1 lb) rabbit fillets
250 g ($\frac{1}{2}$ lb) pork fillets, chopped
250 g ($\frac{1}{2}$ lb) pickled pork, chopped
1 large onion, chopped roughly
1 tablespoon chopped parsley
$\frac{1}{2}$ teaspoon dried thyme
2 cloves garlic, crushed
Salt and black pepper, freshly ground
2 tablespoons red wine
2 tablespoons brandy
4 rashers bacon, rind removed

Take about a quarter of the rabbit fillets and cut
them into strips. Put aside. Chop the remainder of
the rabbit meat, and place in blender with the pork
and onion. Process in the blender until smooth.
Now add the parsley, thyme, garlic, salt, pepper,
wine and brandy. Mix well.

Place half this mixture in a well greased terrine, lay
the rabbit strips on top then cover with the rashers
of bacon. Top with the remainder of the blended
mixture. Cover with foil and stand the terrine in a
roasting dish containing about 2.5 cm (1 in) of
water. Cook in a moderate oven for about two and
a half hours.

Remove from the oven, cool, then place a weight
on top and store in the refrigerator until required.

APPETISER COCKTAILS

Chilled and refreshing, appetiser cocktails are always popular and attractive "starters". Try some of these suggestions. They include delectable combinations of fruit, seafood cocktails with piquant sauce, and of course some wonderful ways with the delicious avocado.

AVOCADO AND SEAFOOD COCKTAIL 1.

3 firm ripe avocados
Lemon juice
3 tablespoons whipped cream *or* mayonnaise
Salt
Cayenne pepper
1 cup flaked salmon *or* crabmeat *or* cooked prawns *or* cooked lobster, chopped
Parsley, chopped finely

Garnish: lemon slices

Cut each avocado in half lengthwise, remove the seed and scoop out most of the flesh with a teaspoon (leaving a firm margin round the skin). Brush the inside of each half with lemon juice to prevent discolouring.
Mash the flesh with a fork and add to the whipped cream or mayonnaise. Season to taste with salt and cayenne pepper. The mixture should be the consistency of whipped cream.
Fold the salmon in lightly and use to fill the avocado shells. Sprinkle the edge of each with some finely chopped parsley and garnish with slices of lemon. Serve well chilled. Serves 6.

AVOCADO AND SEAFOOD COCKTAIL 2.

3 firm, ripe avocados
Lemon juice
3 tablespoons cocktail sauce (p. 33)
1 cup flaked, cooked crab *or* lobster meat *or* prawns.
Lemon wedges for garnishing

Cut each avocado in half lengthwise, remove the seed. Score the avocado flesh with lemon juice to prevent discolouring.
Fold the seafood into the cocktail sauce and spoon into the hollow left by the removal of the seed. Garnish with wedges of lemon and serve well chilled. Serves 6.

AVOCADO AND OYSTER SUPREME

3 ripe avocados
18 oysters, in closed shells
2 hard-boiled eggs
2 tablespoons lemon juice
6 tablespoons olive oil
Salt and pepper

Cut the avocados in halves lengthwise and discard the stones. Allow half an avocado and three oysters for each serve. Open the oysters carefully, retaining the juice. Mash the egg yolk with the back of a wooden spoon, slowly blend in the oyster liquid, lemon juice, oil, salt and pepper to taste. The sauce should be smooth and thick. Just before serving place the oysters in the avocado halves and spoon over the sauce. Serves 6.

GRAPEFRUIT AND AVOCADO

3 grapefruit *or* 2 cans grapefruit segments, drained
3 avocados
Lemon juice
Salt and pepper
Paprika

If using fresh grapefruit, peel, removing all traces of pith and cut into segments. Sweeten slightly, cover and chill.
Cut the avocados in halves lengthwise and remove the stones. Scoop out the flesh with a spoon, mash it then flavour with lemon juice, salt and pepper to taste. Cover and chill. At serving time divide the grapefruit segments between six individual serving dishes and top with spoonsful of the avocado. Sprinkle with paprika before serving. Serves 6.

FRUIT MEDLEY

3 oranges, peeled and sectioned
2 bananas, sliced
2 slices canned *or* fresh pineapple, diced
Lemon juice
Sugar

Combine oranges, bananas and pineapple in a bowl. Sprinkle with lemon juice and sweeten to taste with sugar. Chill. Serve in chilled cocktail glasses or in hollowed-out halves of orange shells. Serves 6.

GOLD COASTER

1 ripe banana, sliced
Lemon juice
2 cups canned fruit cocktail, chilled and drained
1 cup ripe strawberries, washed, hulled, halved and chilled
1 cup cantaloup balls, well chilled
1 small bottle ginger ale
Aromatic bitters (optional)

Dip banana slices in lemon juice to prevent discolouring. Combine with the remaining fruit, cover and chill for several hours. Just before serving pour a little ginger ale over the fruit, and if liked, a dash of aromatic bitters. Spoon into chilled cocktail glasses. Serves 6.

MELON AND PINEAPPLE COCKTAIL

1 cup watermelon balls
1 cup cantaloup balls
470 g (15 oz) can pineapple pieces
½ cup syrup drained from the pineapple
½ cup orange juice
1 tablespoon lemon juice

Garnish: maraschino cherries, mint sprigs

Combine the three fruits in a bowl, cover and chill for several hours. In another container mix the fruit syrup with the fruit juices. At serving time place the fruit in individual serving glasses and spoon over some of the fruit-flavoured syrup. Serve well chilled. Garnish if liked with a maraschino cherry and a mint sprig. Serves 6.

MELON BALL COCKTAILS

Melon balls either alone or in combination with other fruits make an ideal first course. They can be scooped out with a melon baller or a teaspoon. Here are four ideas:
1. Watermelon, cantaloup or honey-dew balls, well chilled and sprinkled with dry ginger ale or dry sherry. Garnish each with a glacé cherry and a mint sprig.
2. Combine ½ a cup of water with ½ a cup of sugar, stir until boiling, then cook for 5 minutes. Cool and add 1 tablespoon of lemon juice and 2 tablespoons of orange juice. Spoon over a combination or any one of the melon balls and garnish with a glacé cherry and a mint sprig.
3. Use papaw instead of melons. Mix with equal quantities of berries (any type). Place in cocktail glasses and sprinkle with lemon juice. Garnish with a glacé cherry and a sprig of mint.
4. Boil ½ a cup of sugar with ½ a cup of water for 5 minutes and pour it over 3 tablespoons of chopped mint. Add 3 tablespoons of lemon juice and 1

Avocado and Seafood Cocktail 2 (p. 31).

Chicken Liver and Mushroom Dip (p. 27), Creamy Chive Dip (p. 26), Guacamole (p. 26).

tablespoon of orange juice. Cover and let stand for 1 hour. Strain, chill and pour it over cubes or balls of papaw.

PAPAW AND BERRY COCKTAIL

1½ cups small cubes *or* balls of papaw
1½ cups quartered strawberries *or* other berries
Lemon juice
Pineapple juice

Garnish: strawberry halves or berries

Combine the papaw cubes or balls with the quartered strawberries. Divide evenly between six cocktail glasses. Sprinkle each with a little lemon juice. Pour about 1 dessertspoon of pineapple juice over each serving before garnishing with the berries. Serve well chilled. Serves 6.

PINEAPPLE MINT COCKTAIL

1 fresh pineapple, peeled, cored and cubed
½ cup sugar
½ cup water
1 cup fresh mint leaves, crushed *or* chopped
1 tablespoon sherry

Garnish: glacé cherries and mint sprigs

Combine the sugar and water in a saucepan, and stir over medium heat until the sugar dissolves and the mixture boils. Boil for 5 minutes. Pour this syrup over the crushed or chopped mint leaves, then cover and let stand until cold. Strain, and add 1 tablespoon of sherry.
Place the pineapple cubes in individual serving dishes and spoon over the liquid, adding a little more sherry if liked. Top each with a glacé cherry and a mint sprig. Serves 6–8.

PEARS IN LIQUEUR

1½ cups fresh orange juice
1½ tablespoons castor sugar
3 tablespoons Curaçao *or* Kirsch *or* Grand Marnier
6 fresh, ripe pears, peeled and quartered *or* diced

Combine the orange juice and sugar, stir until the sugar has dissolved then chill thoroughly. About 15 minutes before serving add the liqueur of your choice and pour over the pears. Serves 6.

STRAWBERRY AND PINEAPPLE COCKTAIL

470 g (15 oz) can cubed pineapple
3 cups fresh strawberries, hulled and washed
¼ cup mint leaves

Garnish: crystallised cherries and mint sprigs

Drain the pineapple, reserving syrup. Place the syrup in a saucepan and bring it to the boil. Pour it over the mint leaves, cover and let stand until cool. Chill the pineapple cubes, the strawberries and the mint syrup.
At serving time, spoon the fruit into cocktail glasses and add some of the minted syrup. Garnish each with a cherry and a sprig of mint. Serves 6.

TOMATO JUICE COCKTAIL

1 large can tomato juice
1 teaspoon Worcestershire sauce
1 teaspoon lemon juice
Whipped cream (optional)

Garnish: lemon wedges and parsley sprigs

Combine the tomato juice, Worcestershire sauce and lemon juice, mixing well. Refrigerate for at least 1 hour. Pour into serving glasses. Top each with a small spoonful of whipped cream if liked. Garnish with lemon wedges and parsley. Serves 6.

SEAFOOD COCKTAILS

Cocktail sauce
¼ cup sweet mayonnaise
½ cup undiluted tomato soup
¼ level teaspoon curry powder
1 teaspoon Worcestershire sauce
1 teaspoon lemon juice
Salt and pepper
¼ cup cream, semi-whipped

Garnish: parsley sprigs, lemon, sliced thinly

Combine the mayonnaise with the tomato soup. Add the next 4 ingredients (quantities can be adjusted to suit your taste). Just before using fold in the semi-whipped cream.

PRAWN COCKTAIL
Line small cocktail glasses with small well-washed and drained lettuce leaves. Arrange shelled prawns in the centre and spoon over the cocktail sauce, using about 2 tablespoonsful for each glass. Garnish with tiny sprigs of parsley and triangles of thinly sliced lemon. Serve well chilled.

WHITEBAIT COCKTAIL
Use freshly cooked or drained, canned whitebait. (To cook fresh whitebait toss it in melted butter in

a pan until the tiny fish have lost their transparent appearance; season with salt and pepper; cool.) Place 1 to 2 tablespoons of the whitebait in each cocktail glass, add about 2 tablespoons of cocktail sauce to each, and garnish with tiny parsley sprigs and thinly sliced lemon triangles.

LOBSTER COCKTAIL

As for whitebait, using chopped cooked lobster.

SEAFOOD COCKTAIL

This may be a combination of any fish, either cooked or canned, and fresh oysters. For each seafood cocktail allow 2 oysters and either 1 prawn or 2 to 3 small shrimps, with 1 tablespoon of salmon and 1 tablespoon of chopped cooked lobster. Spoon over 2 tablespoons of the cocktail sauce and garnish with tiny parsley sprigs and triangles of thinly sliced lemon. Serve well chilled.

CELERY AND SALMON COCKTAIL

Drain and flake 1 pound of canned salmon. Mix with 1 cup of chopped celery. Divide evenly between six cocktail glasses and top each with about 1 tablespoon of cocktail sauce. Garnish with tiny lemon triangles and parsley sprigs.

SOUPS

As every good cook knows the stimulating fragrance of a tempting soup is a perfect prelude to a good meal. And one of the surest tests of a cook is the choice of a soup to complement the rest of the menu. Hearty soups are filling and satisfying before a light meal of eggs or salad; light, piquant soups make an ideal introduction to a meal featuring a roast or other heavy main course. Here is a selection I recommend you try. They'll do all that good soups should—stimulate the appetite, provide nourishment, and taste delicious! They are not difficult to make, and apart from a few standards such as pea soup, cream of mushroom and vegetable soup, they are not the kind you will find in cans.

BASIC STOCKS

500 g (1 lb) beef bones
500 g (1 lb) knuckle of veal
1 large onion, stuck with cloves
2 stalks celery, with top leaves
1 large or two medium sized carrots, chopped roughly
4 sprigs parsley
1 clove garlic (optional)
10 cups cold water
1 teaspoon salt
12 black peppercorns

Beef stock

Place the beef bones, knuckle of veal and the onion in a large saucepan and add the water. Bring slowly to the boil. Lower the heat and simmer for one hour. Add the salt, vegetables, garlic if used, parsley and peppercorns. Simmer for another hour.
Strain into a bowl and cool as quickly as possible (but not in the refrigerator). As soon as the stock cools, cover and store in the refrigerator. Before using remove any surface fat with a slotted spoon. Serves 6.

Chicken Stock

Replace the beef bones and the knuckle of veal with either a boiling fowl, a chicken carcass or some chicken legs. Omit the garlic and reduce the peppercorns by half.

CHICKEN BROTH

1 boiling fowl
1 bouquet garni
2 teaspoons salt
6 cups cold water
2 tablespoons rice
2 stalks celery, chopped finely
2 carrots, scraped and grated
1 onion, peeled and chopped finely
Pepper, freshly ground *or* seasoned
Parsley, chopped

Joint the fowl and place, together with the carcass, in a large saucepan. Add the bouquet garni, salt and cold water and bring very slowly to simmering point. Remove any scum as it rises. Now add the rice and cook for 30 minutes. Prepare the vegetables and add together with a little freshly ground or seasoned pepper. Cover and simmer for a further $1\frac{1}{2}$ hours.

Lift out the chicken pieces. Carefully remove the white meat from the breast bones, chop it into small pieces and return it to the soup. You may use the remainder of the dark meat for chicken patties or rissoles. Skim off any fat from the broth, taste and adjust seasonings and add the parsley.

For special occasions, stir in cream just before serving. Reheat without boiling. Serves 4–6.

CHICKEN WINE SOUP

6 leeks
4 tablespoons melted butter
5 cups chicken stock
1 cup broken macaroni
Rapidly boiling water
1 teaspoon salt
1 clove garlic, cut
1 cup grated Swiss cheese *or* other mild cheese
1 cup white wine

Thoroughly clean the leeks and cut the white part and half the green part into thin slices. Heat the butter in a saucepan, add the leeks and cook over a low heat for about 20 minutes, stirring occasionally to prevent the leeks from browning. Add the chicken stock, cover and cook for 40 minutes longer.

Meanwhile cook the macaroni in a large quantity of boiling water containing the salt and the clove of garlic. The macaroni should take about 20 minutes to become quite tender. Drain, remove the garlic and add the macaroni to the hot soup. Simmer for five minutes longer. Place the Swiss cheese in the top of a double saucepan with the wine. Cook, stirring constantly until the cheese melts completely. Ladle the chicken soup into the hot serving bowls and add a generous tablespoon of the melted cheese and wine to each. Serves 6.

CHICKEN SOUP MAISON

1 boiling fowl
Water
Salt
5 peppercorns
1 bay leaf
2 carrots, scraped and sliced *or* diced
1 parsnip, scraped and sliced *or* diced
1 leek *or* shallots, chopped
2 stalks celery, chopped

Potato Dumplings

$\frac{1}{2}$ to $\frac{3}{4}$ cup cold boiled potato
1 teaspoon salt
1 egg
1 cup plain flour
Nutmeg, grated

Garnish: parsley, chopped

Cut the fowl into eight pieces, place in a large saucepan and cover with cold water. Add the seasonings and the vegetables, cover and simmer for about one hour. While the soup is cooking make the potato dumplings. Mash the potato without any liquid and stir quickly together with the salt, egg, plain flour and grated nutmeg to taste. Take spoonsful and shape into balls about the size of a walnut. Drop them into the boiling soup and cook for 15 minutes. The chicken pieces are removed from the soup before serving. Cut off the white meat from the breasts and cut it into pieces to add to the soup. Serve the soup sprinkled with chopped parsley. Serves 4–6.

Note: From the remaining pieces of cooked chicken carefully remove the meat and use it for a fricassée by combining with white sauce and adding additional flavourings such as hard-boiled egg slices or finely chopped parsley.

OXTAIL SOUP

1 ox tail
Seasoned flour
1 tablespoon butter *or* oil
2 carrots, scraped and sliced
1 large onion, peeled and sliced
2 stalks celery, chopped
1 bouquet garni
2–3 rashers bacon *or* some bacon rind
7 cups stock
1 teaspoon lemon juice *or* 1 tablespoon dry sherry

Divide the ox tail into joints. Blanch them by placing in a saucepan, covering with cold water and bringing to the boil. Strain, then pat the joints dry before rolling them in seasoned flour.

Melt the butter or heat the oil in a large saucepan and add the ox tail pieces. Fry until they are brown on all sides, then lift them out using a slotted spoon and drain on paper to remove the fat. Add the prepared vegetables to the saucepan and fry them lightly until browned. You will probably require to add a little more butter or oil although some will have come from the fat around the ox tail joints. Return the meat to the saucepan and add the bouquet garni, bacon rind or rashers and the stock. Bring slowly to the boil and simmer for at least two hours.

Using a slotted spoon remove the ox tail pieces from the saucepan. Set the soup aside to cool, overnight if necessary. Remove the meat from the bones —if you have cooked it sufficiently it should literally fall off. Shred it finely and add to the soup. When ready to serve remove any fat from the surface of the cooled soup and add either lemon juice or sherry. Bring slowly back to boiling point. Serves 4–6.

Note: For a richer, brown colour a beef soup cube or a few drops of Parisian essence may be added. Serve with sippets.

MINESTRONE

125 g (4 oz) dried kidney *or* haricot beans
125 g (4 oz) salt pork, diced
1 clove garlic, chopped *or* ground
1 small onion, sliced
5 cups cold water *or* stock (add a couple of soup cubes if water is used)
2 carrots, sliced
2 stalks celery, sliced finely
¼ small head cabbage, sliced finely
2–3 tomatoes, chopped
125 g (4 oz) frozen peas
60–90 g (2–3 oz) macaroni
30 g (1 oz) rice
Salt and pepper
2 teaspoons parsley, chopped
2 tablespoons cheese, freshly grated

Soak the beans overnight in cold water. Drain. Cover them with fresh water bring to the boil and simmer for two hours. Put aside. Sauté salt pork in a heavy based saucepan until brown. Add garlic and onion to the pork and sauté for a few minutes. Add the stock, carrot, and celery and bring to the boil. Simmer for a few minutes then add the cabbage and tomato. Reduce heat to bring the soup to a very slow simmer and cook for another one and a half hours.

Twenty minutes before serving add the peas, macaroni and rice and cook until they are tender, about 20 minutes. If the soup is too thick you could add a little water, vegetable stock or beef stock.

Taste and season with salt and pepper and stir in the finely chopped parsley. Serve sprinkled with the grated cheese. Serves 4–6.

PRAWN BISQUE

3 tablespoons butter
1 tablespoon finely chopped shallots
1 tablespoon plain flour
3 cups warm milk
500 g (1 lb) cooked prawns, shelled, de-veined and minced *or* chopped finely
1 cup cream
Salt
Paprika *or* black pepper, freshly ground
Sprinkle of nutmeg
1½ tablespoons dry sherry
1 tablespoon chopped parsley *or* chives

Melt the butter in a good sized saucepan and sauté the shallots until soft but not brown. Now stir in the flour and when it is perfectly smooth cook it without browning for about two minutes. Add the milk and cook, stirring constantly until the soup boils and slightly thickens. Add prawns and cook gently for about five minutes. Pour in the cream, flavour with salt and paprika or pepper and nutmeg. Avoid boiling after the cream has been added. Just before serving add the sherry. Sprinkle each serve with a little parsley or chives. Serve with fried croutons. Serves 4.

VEGETABLE SOUP

1.5 kg (3 lb) beef bones
6 cups cold water
1 teaspoon salt
1 medium onion, peeled and chopped
1 large carrot, scraped and chopped finely
2 stalks celery, chopped
4 ripe tomatoes, peeled and chopped
Salt and pepper
3 tablespoons shell macaroni *or* rice
Parmesan cheese, grated

Place the bones, cold water and salt in a large saucepan and allow to soak for at least half an hour. Cover, place over a low heat and bring slowly to simmering point. Simmer for about half an hour, skimming if necessary. Add the vegetables and cook for a further hour. Lift out the bones, season to taste with salt and pepper and add the macaroni or rice. Cook for a further fifteen minutes.
Serve sprinkled with Parmesan cheese. Serves 4–6.

QUICK VEGETABLE CHOWDER

1 cup shredded lettuce
1 cup finely chopped celery
1 medium onion, chopped
2 medium sized carrots, chopped
2 tablespoons butter
2 cups boiling water
1 or 2 beef stock cubes
½ cup skinned and chopped tomato
1 tablespoon rice
Salt
Paprika

When preparing the lettuce and celery use only the outer leaves and stalks. (Keep the hearts of both to use in salads.) Peel and chop the onion and scrape and chop the carrots.
Melt the butter in a large saucepan, add the prepared vegetables and sauté for about eight minutes tossing to soften all the vegetables evenly.
Add the boiling water, crumbled stock cubes and the tomato. Stir until boiling then add the rice and simmer gently for about 30 minutes. Season lightly with salt and paprika before serving. Serves 4.

CHEESE SOUP

4 medium potatoes, peeled and cubed
1 large onion, peeled and chopped finely
4 cups hot beef stock (made with stock cubes)
250 g (½ lb) Swiss cheese, grated
½ tablespoon grated Parmesan cheese
½ tablespoon chopped shallots or chives
Salt and pepper
½ cup dry white wine
Parsley, chopped

Cook potato and onion in the beef stock until both are soft. Mash with a fork or press through a strainer. Return the soup to the saucepan and add both kinds of cheese and the shallots or chives. Heat slowly, stirring constantly until the mixture is smooth.
Season to taste, but remember that the beef stock made with the stock cubes will be slightly salty. Add the wine and reheat. Top with the chopped parsley and serve with hot, crusty French bread. Serves 4.

FRENCH ONION SOUP

60 g (2 oz) butter
1 tablespoon oil
1 kg (approx. 2 lb) onions, peeled and sliced thinly
1 teaspoon salt
2 tablespoons plain flour
7½ cups boiling stock or half canned consommé and half water
⅔ cup white wine
Brandy (optional)

Croutes

French bread cut into 2.5 cm (1 in) thick slices
Garlic, crushed
60 to 90 g (2–3 oz) cheese, grated
60 to 90 g (2–3 oz) Parmesan cheese, grated

Melt the butter in a heavy based saucepan and add the oil. Add the onions and salt to the saucepan and cook until the onions are golden in colour. Stir as they cook to ensure even browning, this should take about 20 minutes. Sprinkle in the flour and cook, stirring lightly, for about three minutes. Remove the saucepan from the heat and add the boiling stock and then the wine. Season to taste, cover and simmer for 30 or 40 minutes. Skim if necessary. Taste for seasoning and, if liked, add two tablespoons of brandy for extra flavor.
While the soup is cooking make the croutes.
Place the bread slices in a single layer in a shallow pan and bake for about 15 minutes at 160° C (325° F). Brush the slices with olive oil, turn them over and bake for a further 15 minutes or until the bread is crusty and lightly browned.
If a light garlic flavor is desired add a mashed clove of garlic to the oil as the slices are turned over.

To serve

Place a slice of the browned bread in each serving dish and pour over it the hot soup. Mix the cheeses and sprinkle over each dish. Place the bowls either in a moderate oven or under the griller to melt and lightly brown the cheese. Serve immediately. Serves 6.

CARROT VICHYSSOISE

4 medium potatoes, peeled and sliced
4 large carrots, scraped and sliced
2 large leeks, sliced
750 g (1½ lb) ham or bacon bones
5 cups chicken stock
1 teaspoon sugar
Black pepper, freshly gound
Salt
1 cup cream

Garnish: raw carrot, freshly grated

Place the potatoes, carrots and leeks, ham or bacon bones, and chicken stock in a saucepan cover and bring slowly to the boil. Simmer until the vegetables are quite soft. Remove bones.

Rub soup through a sieve or purée in a blender.
Return the soup to the saucepan and add the sugar, pepper and salt to taste. Stir in the cream and reheat without boiling.
Serve with a garnish of freshly grated carrot. Serves 6.

FRESH TOMATO SOUP

TRY

1 kg (2 lb) ripe tomatoes, chopped roughly
2 tablespoons cold water
2½ cups beef stock
Salt and pepper
¼ teaspoon sugar
1 cob corn
2 tablespoons chopped shallot
Parsley, chopped finely (optional)

Wash the tomatoes, chop them roughly and place in a saucepan with the cold water. Cover and cook over a low heat until they are pulpy. This should take about 15 minutes. Rub them through a sieve to remove the skin and seeds.
Return the pulp to the saucepan and add the beef stock. Bring to the boil then season to taste with salt and pepper and add the sugar. Cook the corn on the cob for about 15 minutes in unsalted water. Drain, scrape the kernels from the cob and add to the soup.
Sauté the shallots in a little butter and stir into the soup just before serving. A sprinkling of chopped parsley may be added to each serve. Serves 4.

POTAGE ROSE

4 cups beef stock *or* 3 cups consommé and 1 cup water
90 g (6 oz) tomato paste
2 tablespoons very finely chopped celery leaves
2 tablespoons very finely chopped shallot leaves
Pinch thyme
1 bay leaf
1½ tablespoons cornflour
¼ cup Madeira or port
2 egg yolks
1 cup cream
Salt and pepper
1 tablespoon butter

Place stock in a large saucepan with the tomato paste, celery leaves, onion tops, thyme and bay leaf. Cover, bring to the boil then lower the heat and simmer for about half an hour to blend the flavours.
Blend the cornflour with a little cold water to make a smooth paste. Add a little of the hot soup to this mixture, blend it thoroughly then stir slowly into the soup. Add the wine and stir until the soup boils and thickens slightly. Blend the egg yolks with the cream. Remove the soup from the heat, add a little of the hot soup to the egg mixture and blend

thoroughly before stirring the egg mixture into the saucepan. Taste, adding salt and pepper if necessary and serve with a little pat of butter floating in each bowl. Serves 4.

GOLDEN PUMPKIN SOUP

1 kg (2 lb) dry pumpkin, peeled, seeded and cut into chunks
1 medium onion, chopped
3¾ cups good chicken stock
2 teaspoons sugar
Pinch pepper
Pinch nutmeg
Pinch cinnamon
½ cup milk
Salt
Whipped cream
Nutmeg

Place pumpkin and onion in a large saucepan and pour over the stock. Cover, bring to the boil then simmer for about 40 minutes or until the pumpkin is soft enough to purée either in a blender or through a sieve.
Return the soup to the saucepan and, stirring occasionally to prevent it sticking, bring to almost boiling. Add the milk, sugar, pepper, cinnamon and nutmeg. At this stage taste and add salt as required. Reheat, this time without boiling. Serve very hot, topping each serve with a spoonful of whipped cream which has been very lightly sprinkled with nutmeg. Serves 4.

PUMPKIN AND APPLE SOUP

2 kg (4–5 lb) pumpkin, peeled, seeded and cut into chunks
2 onions, sliced
2 cooking apples, peeled and sliced
4 cups water
3 bacon stock cubes, crumbled
1 teaspoon nutmeg
Salt and pepper
2 rashers of bacon cut into 2.5 cm (1 in) pieces
4 thin frankfurters, sliced diagonally
½ cup cream

Place pumpkin, onion and apple in a heavy based saucepan with the water, stock cubes, nutmeg and salt and pepper to taste. Bring slowly to the boil then simmer for about 40 minutes. Cool slightly then put through a blender or force through a sieve. Return the soup to the saucepan and reheat.
Sauté the bacon pieces and the frankfurters in a pan until the bacon fat is clear and the frankfurters lightly browned. Lift out and drain on absorbent paper. Add to the soup. Just before serving stir in the cream. Reheat but do not allow to boil. Serves 4.

LEEK AND PUMPKIN SOUP

1 large onion, chopped
500 g (1 lb) pumpkin, peeled, seeded and diced
250 g (½ lb) potatoes, peeled and diced
2 tablespoons butter
250 g (½ lb) fresh *or* canned haricot *or* broad beans
2½ cups milk
Salt and cayenne pepper
60 g (2 oz) leek, sliced thinly
2½ cups chicken stock
1 cup cream
125 g (4 oz) rice, boiled
1 tablespoon chopped chervil *or* parsley *or* 2 tablespoons
    crisply fried and chopped *or* crumbled bacon

Sauté onion in half the butter until soft but not brown. Add the pumpkin, potatoes, fresh (not canned) beans and milk and bring slowly to the boil.

Cover and simmer for about 45 minutes, or until the vegetables are soft enough to purée through a sieve or in a blender. If canned beans are used, add them at the end of the cooking. As this soup is made with a milk base it will be necessary to stir it occasionally during the simmering process to prevent it sticking.

When it has been puréed replace the soup in the saucepan and season to taste with salt and pepper.

Melt remaining butter in pan, add leeks and cook gently until soft. Add them to the soup together with the chicken stock. Bring slowly to the boil and just before serving stir in the cream and the freshly boiled rice.

Serve topped with the chervil or parsley or the crisply fried chopped or crumbled bacon. Serves 4–6.

LEEK AND POTATO SOUP

4 leeks
1 small white onion, minced finely
2 tablespoons butter
4 potatoes, peeled and cubed
4 cups chicken stock (or water and 2 soup cubes)
1 teaspoon salt
White pepper
1 cup cream *or* half milk and half cream
Croutons and either Parmesan cheese, grated *or* chives,
    chopped

Cut the green part from the leeks. Reserve them to use in another dish as only the white stalks are necessary for this soup. Slice white part of leeks thinly and place in a saucepan with the butter and the onion. Cook for a few minutes or until both the onion and leek begin to soften. On no account allow them to brown. Now add the potatoes and sauté for a few minutes. Add the chicken stock, the salt, and a little white pepper. The amount of salt used will depend

on the saltiness of the stock. Use it sparingly at this stage, you can always add more before serving.

Cover, bring to the boil and simmer until the vegetables are soft enough to press through a sieve or purée in a blender. Return the soup to the saucepan and add the cream. Reheat without boiling and correct the seasonings. Serve with croutons and a sprinkling of either cheese or chives. Serves 4–6.

Note: For a richer soup one or two egg yolks may be blended with the cream before adding to the soup. Take care not to allow it to boil after the egg yolks have been added.

POTAGE PARMENTIER

4 large potatoes, peeled and diced
2 leeks *or* large onions, chopped
7 cups cold water
Salt and pepper
2 tablespoons chopped parsley *or* 1 tablespoon chopped
    chives
1 cup milk *or* ½ cup milk and ½ cup cream
2 tablespoons butter

Place potatoes and leeks in a large saucepan. Add water and season with salt and pepper. Cover and bring to the boil. Reduce heat and simmer the soup for about 45 minutes or until vegetables are quite soft.

Press through a strainer or use a blender and return the soup to the saucepan and add the parsley or chives. Thin down with the milk or milk and cream and add the butter. Serve piping hot, well seasoned with additional salt and pepper. Serves 6.

MUSHROOM CHOWDER

4 tablespoons rice
1½ cups meat stock
⅓ cup butter
375 g (¾ lb) mushrooms, sliced thinly
1 large onion, peeled and chopped
4 cups boiling stock
½ cup grated raw carrot
¾ cup small cubed potato
½ cup finely chopped celery
Salt, pepper and cayenne
Parsley, chopped
Grated nutmeg
Whipped cream

Soak the rice in the meat stock for at least one hour. Melt the butter in a large saucepan and add the thinly sliced mushrooms and onion. Cook for about five minutes. Stir in the boiling stock. Bring to the boil and add the carrot, potato cubes, celery and undrained rice. Bring the soup to the boil again and simmer for about 40 minutes or until the rice is quite soft. Season to taste with salt, pepper and cayenne. It should be served piping hot, topped with a sprinkling of finely chopped parsley and a little grated nutmeg then a spoonful of whipped cream floated on the surface. Serves 4–6.

Golden Pumpkin Soup (p. 39).

Chicken Liver Terrine (p. 29).

CREAM OF MUSHROOM SOUP

5 cups sliced mushrooms
$\frac{1}{4}$ medium sized onion, peeled and sliced
$1\frac{1}{2}$ tablespoons butter
2 teaspoons plain flour
$\frac{1}{2}$ teaspoon each salt and thyme
$\frac{1}{4}$ teaspoon pepper
2 teaspoons tomato paste
2 teaspoons lemon juice
4 cups milk

Sauté the mushrooms and onions in the butter until both are tender, about two minutes. Add the flour, salt, thyme and pepper and cook for about two minutes. Blend in the tomato paste, lemon juice and one cup of the milk. Pour into the blender and process until puréed. Return the mixture to the saucepan, add the remainder of the milk and stir until the soup comes to the boil. Simmer gently for a few minutes. Serve with sippets. Serves 4–6.

CORN CHOWDER

2 slices bacon, diced
4 small onions, chopped
6 medium potatoes, peeled and cubed
2 teaspoons salt
$\frac{1}{4}$ teaspoon pepper
$2\frac{1}{2}$ cups boiling water
1 large can corn kernels
4 tomatoes, peeled and sliced
$\frac{1}{4}$ teaspoon bi-carbonate of soda
30 g (1 oz) flour
5 cups milk
1 tablespoon butter
Parsley, chopped
Bacon, fried crisply and crumbled

Fry bacon until lightly brown and crisp. Remove from the pan. Add the onion and potatoes to the fat left in the pan, season with salt and pepper and add the boiling water. Cover and simmer until the vegetables are almost tender then add the corn and tomatoes. Cook for 10 minutes.
Blend the flour with a little of the cold milk then add the remainder of the milk, the soda and the butter. Stir into the soup and continue to stir over a medium heat until the mixture boils and slightly thickens. Simmer for five minutes.
Place a little chopped parsley and fried bacon in a soup plate before adding the chowder. Serve with toast sippets and, if liked, snippets of pimento. Serves 6.

CURRIED CREAM OF CORN SOUP

4 cups cooked corn kernels, either fresh *or* frozen
$\frac{1}{4}$ medium sized onion, peeled and sliced
1 tablespoon butter
1 tablespoon flour
$\frac{3}{4}$ teaspoon curry powder
$\frac{1}{4}$ teaspoon salt
Pinch pepper
2 cups chicken stock
2 cups milk

Sauté the corn and onion in the butter for about two minutes or until the corn is just tender. Stir in the flour, curry powder, salt and pepper. Cook over a medium heat, stirring constantly for a few minutes but do not allow the flour to brown. Gradually stir in the chicken stock and cook for a further two minutes. Pour into the blender and blend until smooth. Add the milk and stir constantly over a medium heat until the soup barely boils. Serves 6.

CREAM OF BROCCOLI SOUP

$2\frac{1}{2}$ cups chicken broth
750 g ($1\frac{1}{2}$ lb) frozen broccoli
1 bay leaf
$\frac{1}{4}$ cup butter
$\frac{1}{4}$ cup plain flour
$\frac{1}{4}$ teaspoon salt
Seasoned pepper
2 cups milk
Chives *or* parsley, chopped

Combine the chicken broth and broccoli in a saucepan and add the bay leaf. Cover, bring to the boil then lower the heat and simmer for about five minutes or until the broccoli is tender.
Meanwhile in another saucepan melt the butter, add the flour, salt and pepper and stir until smooth. Cook for one or two minutes without browning, add the milk and stir over a medium heat until the soup boils and slightly thickens.
Remove from the heat, lift out the bay leaf and transfer the soup to a blender. Blend until the soup is smooth. Add the white sauce, blend again. Before serving bring the soup to just below boiling point. Sprinkle with chopped chives or parsley and serve with fried sippets. Serves 4–6.

Variation

As a variation from the sippets and chives or parsley garnish you may like to serve lemon croutons. To make them, cut some stale white bread into cubes. Melt about two tablespoons of butter in a frying pan and add one teaspoon of grated lemon rind. Add a cup of the bread cubes and cook over a medium heat, stirring constantly until the bread cubes are crisp and a golden brown colour.

CREAM OF SPINACH SOUP

1 bunch spinach
2 tablespoons finely chopped onion
3 tablespoons butter
3 tablespoons plain flour
1½ cups milk
Salt
Pepper
Nutmeg
Cayenne pepper
2 egg yolks
¾ cup cream
1 tablespoon finely chopped parsley

Wash the spinach leaves and trim the stems. Place in a saucepan with about one cup of water and a little salt and cook for about 15 or 20 minutes or until the leaves are soft. Drain, reserve the liquid, and purée the spinach by pressing through a sieve or processing in the blender. Place the onion and butter in a saucepan and sauté until the onion just begins to colour, stirring constantly. Add the flour and blend until smooth, cook for two minutes without browning and add the milk. Cook, stirring constantly until the soup boils and slightly thickens.
Strain through a fine sieve into another saucepan and add the purée and the spinach liquid. Season to taste with salt, pepper, nutmeg and cayenne. Simmer gently for about five minutes, stirring occasionally.
In a small bowl beat the egg yolks with the cream and add gradually to the spinach soup stirring constantly. Stir in the parsley just before serving.
You may prefer fried croutons to the parsley. If so, melt about two tablespoons of butter in a pan and add a cup of small bread cubes. Cook, stirring constantly until they are a uniform brown colour. Serves 4.

CREAM OF CAULIFLOWER SOUP

1 medium size cauliflower
60 g (2 oz) butter or bacon fat
2 tablespoons chopped shallot
2 tablespoons plain flour
5 cups chicken stock
½ cup milk
2 egg yolks
½ cup cream
1 teaspoon lemon juice
Salt and pepper
Nutmeg (optional)

Remove the leaves and thick stalks from the cauliflower and break the head into flowerlets. Set aside about twelve tiny flowerlets to use as a garnish.
Melt the butter or bacon fat in a saucepan, add the shallots and cook until soft but not brown. Add the flour, stir until smooth then cook without browning for about two minutes. Add the chicken stock and

stir constantly until the soup comes to the boil. Add the cauliflower, cover and simmer until the vegetables are soft enough to rub through a sieve or purée in a blender.
While the soup is cooking place the reserved flowerlets in a saucepan containing boiling salted water and cook until soft. Drain, then run cold water through to prevent them becoming softer. Set aside.
Purée the soup, return it to the saucepan and add the milk. Beat the egg yolks with the cream and stir into the mixture about one cup of the hot soup. Slowly stir this mixture into the main body of the soup. When thoroughly blended add the lemon juice.
Add the tiny flowerlets, heat but do not boil, then check the seasonings adding a dash of nutmeg if liked. Serves 6–8.

SWEDISH CAULIFLOWER SOUP

1 kg (2 lb) cauliflower
60 g (2 oz) butter
2 rounded tablespoons plain flour
Salt and pepper
5 cups stock or water and two soup cubes
2 egg yolks
½ cup cream
1 tablespoon minced parsley

Wash the cauliflower and break into flowerlets removing any tough stems. Place in a large saucepan, cover with water and add one teaspoon of salt. Cook until soft, about 15 or 20 minutes. Drain well then beat the cauliflower to a pulp. Set aside.
Melt the butter in a saucepan, add the flour, salt and pepper to taste and stir until smooth. Cook for one or two minutes without browning. Add the stock and cook, stirring constantly until the mixture boils and slightly thickens. Cook for two or three minutes. Meanwhile blend the egg yolks and cream in a bowl, pour on a little of the hot soup, stir until smooth then return the mixture to the saucepan. Bring to just below boiling point. Stir in the pulped cauliflower and the parsley. Reheat before serving. Serve immediately accompanied with sippets. Serves 4–6.

GREEK LEMON SOUP

⅓ cup rice
6 cups chicken stock
2 egg yolks
Juice one lemon

Wash the rice in several changes of cold water to thoroughly remove any loose starch. Drain thoroughly. Place the chicken stock in a saucepan, add the rice and cook for 30 or 40 minutes or until the rice is quite soft.
Whisk the egg yolks with the lemon juice then gradually pour on one cup of the hot broth, stirring constantly. Remove the chicken broth from the heat, add the egg mixture then reheat without boiling. Serve very hot. Serves 4.

PEA SOUP

1 cup split peas
8 cups cold water
1 ham bone *or* some bacon bones
2 beef bones
Salt
12 peppercorns
1 blade mace
1 large carrot, chopped
1 onion, chopped
1 parsnip, chopped
5 stalks celery, chopped
1 teaspoon dried mint
2 tablespoons plain flour

Soak the peas overnight in some of the cold water. Next day place them in a large saucepan with the remainder of the water, the ham bone, beef bones, $\frac{1}{2}$ teaspoon salt, peppercorns and mace. Cover and bring slowly to simmering point.

Add the vegetables to the saucepan and continue to cook for about three hours.

Lift out the bones and purée the soup by rubbing through a sieve or processing in a blender, about a cupful at a time. Return the soup to the saucepan and add the mint. Bring to the boil and then bind the mixture with the flour which has been blended to a smooth paste with a little cold water. Simmer for a further five minutes. Taste and add salt as required. Serve with fried sippets. Serves 6.

ENTREES

One of the most treasured possessions in my library of cookbooks is one published fifty years ago. It leans heavily on French cuisine and on the subject of cold entrees says: "Cold Entrees are much in favour in the Dinner Menu in hot weather, and are served also at Balls or Dance Suppers, Banquets, Shooting Party Luncheons, Wedding Receptions, Smart Luncheons etc." How much simpler is our catering today!

Entrees both hot and cold still have a place in some of our more formal menus but now we usually think of them as light luncheon or supper dishes.

The choice is wide and the methods of cooking varied, but basically the original idea of the entree remains the same. That is, the dish should be complete in itself, although we do, when using the entree as a luncheon dish, often accompany it with vegetables.

Here's a collection of some of my favourites.

OYSTERS FLORENTINE

3 dozen oysters on half shell
1 cup puréed, cooked spinach
1½ teaspoons very finely chopped shallot
1 clove garlic, crushed
1½ tablespoons Worcestershire sauce
Salt and pepper
Cracker crumbs
3 tablespoons melted butter
Parmesan cheese, grated

Mix the spinach, shallot, garlic and sauce. Season with salt and pepper and add a few cracker crumbs to take up any excess juice. Stir in the melted butter. Lift the oysters from the shells, add a spoonful of the spinach mixture to each shell and top with an oyster. Sprinkle with the Parmesan cheese and bake in a hot oven for about 10 minutes or until the oysters are plumped.

OYSTERS KILPATRICK

3 dozen oysters on half shell
3 bacon rashers, chopped finely
3½ tablespoons Worcestershire sauce
3½ tablespoons lemon juice
3½ tablespoons tomato sauce *or* sherry

Garnish: parsley

Chop the bacon finely. Divide between the three dozen oysters. Combine the sauce, lemon juice and tomato sauce or sherry and place about a teaspoonful on each oyster. Grill the oysters until the bacon is crisp on top. Serve with a parsley garnish.

OYSTER MORNAY

30 g (1 oz) butter
2 teaspoons chopped shallot
2 level tablespoons plain flour
$\frac{1}{2}$ teaspoon salt
$\frac{1}{2}$ teaspoon dry mustard
$\frac{1}{8}$ teaspoon cayenne pepper
1 cup milk
Lemon juice
2 teaspoons mayonnaise
2 dozen oysters
2 tablespoons soft white breadcrumbs
2 tablespoons cheese, grated

Garnish: lemon wedges and parsley sprigs

Melt the butter in a saucepan and sauté the shallot until soft but not brown. Add the flour, salt, mustard and cayenne pepper and stir until smooth. Cook for 1 minute without browning. Add the milk and stir until the sauce boils and thickens. Simmer for 2 minutes, then add 1 teaspoon of lemon juice and the mayonnaise.
Place a spoonful of this sauce in each of six lightly greased ramekin dishes or scallop shells. Top each with 4 well-drained oysters, then spoon over the remainder of the sauce. Sprinkle the top with breadcrumbs and grated cheese and bake in a moderate oven, 180° C (350° F), until the top browns and the sauce bubbles. Serve with lemon wedges and parsley sprigs.

ASPARAGUS CASSEROLE

439 g (15$\frac{1}{2}$ oz) can asparagus spears
1 medium-sized green pepper
3 eggs
1 teaspoon salt
$\frac{1}{4}$ teaspoon pepper
$\frac{3}{4}$ cup soft white breadcrumbs
1 cup Cheddar cheese cut into 3 mm ($\frac{1}{4}$ in) cubes
1 cup milk
1$\frac{1}{2}$ tablespoons butter *or* margarine

Garnish: tomato slices and parsley sprigs

Drain the asparagus and cut the spears into pieces about 5 cm (2 in) in length. Remove the seeds from the green pepper and cut it into small pieces.
Beat the eggs well and add the salt, pepper, breadcrumbs, green pepper, cheese and milk. Add the asparagus. Pour into a 4 cup capacity casserole or a 23 cm (9 in) tart plate. Melt the butter and pour over the top.
Bake uncovered in a moderate oven, 180° C (350° F), until the custard has set—about 30 to 40 minutes. Serve warm, garnished with fresh tomato slices and sprigs of parsley.
This casserole may be made in advance and reheated. It is substantial enough to serve as a main luncheon dish. Serves 4.

ASPARAGUS CHEESE BAKE

439 g (15$\frac{1}{2}$ oz) can asparagus spears
8 slices ham
30 g (1 oz) butter
2 teaspoons chopped onion
1 tablespoon chopped green pepper
2 level tablespoons plain flour
$\frac{1}{2}$ teaspoon salt
Pinch cayenne pepper
$\frac{1}{2}$ teaspoon mustard
1$\frac{1}{4}$ cups milk
$\frac{1}{4}$ teaspoon Worcestershire sauce
90 g (3 oz) grated cheese

Topping: 1 tablespoon grated cheese

Drain the asparagus well, place 2 spears on each piece of ham and roll up. Arrange in a greased casserole dish.
Melt the butter in a saucepan and sauté the onion and green pepper until soft but not brown. Stir in the flour and cook for a few more minutes, then season with the salt, cayenne and mustard. Add the milk and stir until the sauce boils and thickens.
Cook for 2 minutes, then add the Worcestershire sauce and the grated cheese. Stir until the cheese melts.
Pour the sauce over the rolls and sprinkle with the extra cheese. Bake in a moderate oven, 180° C (350° F), for about 20 minutes or until the cheese on top melts and browns and the sauce bubbles. Serves 4.

ASPARAGUS CREAM RAMEKINS

1$\frac{1}{2}$ tablespoons butter
3 level tablespoons plain flour
$\frac{1}{2}$ teaspoon salt
Pinch pepper
1 teaspoon mustard
1$\frac{1}{2}$ cups milk
439 g (15$\frac{1}{2}$ oz) can asparagus spears
2 tablespoons cream
3 hard-boiled eggs, chopped
$\frac{1}{2}$ cup chopped ham
$\frac{1}{2}$ cup grated cheese
1 cup fried bread cubes

Melt the butter and add the flour, salt, pepper and mustard. Stir over medium heat until smooth, then cook for 1 minute. Add the milk and stir until the sauce boils and thickens. Drain the liquid from the asparagus and add about $\frac{1}{4}$ cup to the sauce, then add the cream (if preferred, omit the cream and increase the quantity of asparagus liquid by 2 tablespoonsful). Fold in hard-boiled eggs, ham, and the asparagus which has been cut into 25 mm (1 in) pieces.
Spoon the mixture into lightly greased ramekins, sprinkle the tops with grated cheese, then add the fried bread cubes. Bake in a hot oven, 220° C (425° F), until the sauce is bubbly. Serves 4–6.

ASPARAGUS HAM AU GRATIN

60 g (2 oz) butter *or* margarine
¼ cup plain flour
¼ teaspoon dry mustard
¼ teaspoon salt
Pinch cayenne pepper
2 cups milk
1 cup chopped cooked ham
2 cups soft white breadcrumbs
1 medium-sized can asparagus
1 cup shredded cheese

Melt the butter in a saucepan and add the flour, mustard, salt and pepper. Stir until smooth, then cook for 1 minute without browning. Add the milk and stir until the sauce boils and thickens. Remove from the heat and add the ham.
Spread 1 cup of the breadcrumbs in the bottom of a greased casserole dish. Add half the drained asparagus, half the cheese, then the remainder of the asparagus. Cover with the creamed ham, top with the rest of the breadcrumbs then with the remaining cheese.
Bake in a moderate oven, 180° C (350° F), for about 30 minutes or until the sauce bubbles and the top is lightly browned. Serves 4–6.

TOAST ROLLS WITH HAM AND ASPARAGUS

1 439 g (15½ oz) can asparagus
8 thin slices fresh bread
Melted butter
8 slices cooked ham
Cream sauce

Drain the liquid from the asparagus and retain it for the cream sauce. Remove the crusts from the bread and brush each slice on both sides with melted butter.
Place a slice of ham and a few asparagus spears on each slice of bread. Roll up, enclosing the asparagus and fasten with wooden toothpicks.
Place on a shallow tray which has been lightly greased and bake in a hot oven 200° C (400° F) until they are lightly browned. Mask with cream sauce and serve.

Sauce

1 tablespoon butter
1½ tablespoons plain flour
½ cup milk
½ cup liquid drained from asparagus
Salt and pepper

Melt the butter in a small saucepan, add the flour and stir until smooth. Cook for one or two minutes without browning then add the milk and asparagus liquid and cook, stirring constantly until the sauce boils and thickens. Season to taste with salt and pepper. Makes 8 rolls.

ASPARAGUS SAVOURY

439 g (15½ oz) can asparagus spears
4 hard-boiled eggs, sliced
2 cups sliced cooked potatoes
2 rashers bacon, crisped
2 teaspoons butter
1½ tablespoons plain flour
¼ teaspoon salt
Pinch pepper
1½ cups milk
¼ cup grated cheese
2 tablespoons buttered breadcrumbs

Garnish: parsley

Cut the well-drained asparagus spears into 5 cm (2 in) lengths and place in a lightly greased casserole. Cover with a layer of hard-boiled egg, then with a layer of sliced cooked potato. Sprinkle with the cooked and crumbled bacon.
Make a white sauce by melting the butter and adding the plain flour, salt and pepper. Stir until smooth, then cook without browning for 1 minute. Add the milk and cook while stirring well until the sauce boils and thickens. Simmer for 3 minutes. Pour over the ingredients in the casserole and sprinkle with the grated cheese and buttered breadcrumbs.
Bake at 180° C (350° F) for about 20 minutes or until the top is browned and the mixture bubbles. Serve garnished with parsley.

POTATO ROLL WITH MUSHROOM FILLING

2½ tablespoons butter
3 eggs, separated
3 to 4 tablespoons sour cream
3 level tablespoons self-raising flour
Pinch salt
1 medium-sized potato, boiled and grated
Dry breadcrumbs

Filling

1 medium-sized onion, chopped
2 tablespoons melted butter *or* oil
250 g (½ lb) fresh mushrooms, sliced
Salt and pepper
2 eggs

Cream the butter and add the egg yolks one at a time, creaming well with each addition, then add the sour cream, the sifted flour and salt and the potato. Beat the egg whites stiffly and fold into the mixture.
Grease a Swiss roll tin well with butter and sprinkle with breadcrumbs. Spread the potato mixture evenly in the tin. Bake at 180° C (350° F) for 30 minutes. Turn out and, while still hot, roll up like a Swiss roll. Unroll, fill with the mushroom filling, re-roll, and serve sliced.
To make the filling, chop the onion and fry it in the heated butter or oil until soft but not brown; add

sliced mushrooms and cook until soft, seasoning with salt and pepper. Beat the eggs, add to the mixture and cook, stirring with a wooden spoon until the mixture resembles scrambled eggs. Serves 4.

SWEET CORN AND GREEN PEA RAMEKINS

1 medium-sized can kernel-style sweet corn
1 cup white sauce
1 cup cooked and drained green peas
1 tablespoon chopped red *or* green pepper
1 teaspoon chopped shallot
2 rashers bacon

Drain the liquid from the sweet corn. Mix the corn with the white sauce and add the peas and the chopped pepper and shallot.
Remove the rind from the bacon, and cut each rasher in half, then roll and secure each piece with a skewer or a cocktail pick.
Divide the sweet corn mixture between four lightly greased ramekins. Top each with a bacon roll. Bake in a moderate oven, 180° C (350° F), for about 15 minutes or until the sauce bubbles and the bacon is cooked. Serves 4.

CAULIFLOWER A LA POLONAISE

1 medium-sized cauliflower
Boiling salted water
125 g (4 oz) butter
⅓ cup fine dry breadcrumbs
1 hard-boiled egg, cooled and chopped

Garnish: parsley sprigs

Break the cauliflower into flowerlets and soak for 10 minutes in cold water. Drain and place in a large saucepan of boiling salted water. Cover and cook for about 10 minutes or until the stems are fork tender. Drain carefully and place in a lightly greased oven-proof dish.
Heat the butter in a saucepan until it bubbles then pour half over the cauliflower. Stir the breadcrumbs into the remaining butter and when completely absorbed add the chopped egg. Mix lightly then sprinkle over the cauliflower. Reheat in a moderate oven 180° C (350° F) and serve with a parsley sprig garnish. Serves 6.

SPINACH CRÊPES WITH SPICY TOMATO SAUCE

Crêpes
6 tablespoons plain flour
½ teaspoon salt
3 tablespoons melted butter
2 eggs
1 cup milk
2 tablespoons brandy

Filling
1 packet frozen spinach
1 tablespoon butter
Salt and black pepper, freshly ground
250 g (½ lb) ricotta cheese
1 egg, lightly beaten
Parmesan cheese, freshly grated
4 tablespoons cream
Nutmeg, freshly grated

Sauce
4 rashers rindless bacon, rind removed and diced
2 onions, peeled and chopped finely
2 cloves garlic, peeled and crushed
1 large can peeled tomatoes
½ teaspoon basil
½ teaspoon oregano
1 bay leaf
½ cup beef stock
1 tablespoon cornflour
¼ cup red wine
1 teaspoon sugar
½ teaspoon salt
¼ teaspoon pepper
Worcestershire sauce (optional)

Make the sauce first. Sauté bacon over a medium heat until it is crisp. Lift from the pan with a slotted spoon and drain on paper. Add the onions, garlic, tomatoes, basil, oregano, bay leaf and stock. Bring to the boil, cover and simmer for about 30 minutes. In a small bowl blend the cornflour with the wine and add the sugar.
Remove the bay leaf from the tomato mixture before rubbing through a sieve. Return the mixture to the saucepan and add the blended mixture. Stir until it boils and thickens. Add the bacon, taste and adjust the seasonings if necessary. If liked a little Worcestershire sauce could be added for extra flavour.

Sift the flour and salt for the crepes into a bowl. Beat the eggs lightly and add the milk and melted butter. Make a well in the centre of the flour, add the liquid then, using the back of a wooden stirring spoon, gradually draw in the dry flour from the sides and beat until you have a smooth batter about the consistency of cream. Add the brandy. Cover and set aside for at least one hour, preferably two.
To cook the crepes, heat about two tablespoons of butter in a well heated heavy based pan. spoon in about two tablespoons of the batter then tilt the pan to allow the batter to spread evenly. Cook over a medium heat until the underside is golden in colour,

47

then turn and cook on the other side. Lift out on to a hot plate. Continue in this way until all the batter has been used, stacking the crêpes one on top of the other as they cook.

Thaw the spinach and place it in a saucepan with the butter. Cook for about five minutes. Season to taste with salt and pepper. Drain well and add the ricotta, the beaten egg, one or two tablespoons of Parmesan cheese, the cream and the nutmeg.

Spread each crêpe with a generous portion of the spinach filling and roll up. Place the filled crêpes side by side in a well buttered ovenproof dish and chill for about one hour. When nearing serving time, brush the crêpes with melted butter and sprinkle with Parmesan cheese.

Bake in a moderate oven 180° C (350° F) for about 20 minutes. Serve two or three to each guest with a few spoonsful of the sauce poured over the top. Serves 6.

FRESH CORN SOUFFLÉ

2 tablespoons butter
1 tablespoon finely chopped onion
2½ tablespoons plain flour
1 teaspoon salt
Pinch pepper
¾ cup milk
2 cups freshly cooked corn, scraped from the cob
5 eggs, separated

Melt the butter in a saucepan and sauté the onion until soft but not brown. Stir in the flour, salt and pepper. Cook, stirring well, for 1 minute (do not allow to brown). Remove from the heat, add the milk, and return the saucepan to the heat. Stir until the sauce boils and thickens, then add the corn and cook for a further minute.

Remove from the heat, add the egg yolks, return the pan to the heat and cook for a few seconds.

Place the egg whites in a warm, dry bowl, add a pinch of salt and beat until stiff. Fold half into the sauce, then lightly stir in the remainder.

Turn the mixture into a greased soufflé dish and bake in a moderate oven. 180° C (350° F), for 40 to 45 minutes. Serve immediately. Serves 4.

ASPARAGUS SOUFFLÉ

1 small can asparagus spears
2 teaspoons butter

Sauce

1 cup milk *or* half milk and half asparagus liquid
4 thin slices onion
1 bayleaf
1 clove
1½ tablespoons butter
1½ slightly rounded tablespoons plain flour
Salt and pepper
Nutmeg
Paprika
3 eggs, separated

Drain the liquid from the asparagus spears, place them in a saucepan with the 2 teaspoons of butter and sauté over medium heat until hot. Keep hot while you make the soufflé sauce.

Place the milk in a saucepan with the onion, bayleaf and clove and bring to the boil. Strain and cool.

Melt the 1½ tablespoons butter and add the flour. Stir until smooth, then cook for 1 minute without browning. Add the strained milk, season with salt, pepper, nutmeg and paprika to taste and stir until the sauce boils and thickens. Cook for 2 minutes. Add the egg yolks, and cook for another minute. Beat the egg whites until soft peaks form, then fold into the sauce.

Place the hot asparagus spears in a greased soufflé dish and pour over the soufflé sauce. Bake at 180° C (350° F) for 35 to 40 minutes. Serve immediately. Serves 4.

TOMATO CHEESE SOUFFLÉ

1 bayleaf
4 thin slices onion
1 clove
¾ cup milk
1 tablespoon butter
2 tablespoons plain flour
½ cup tomato purée *or* soup
¼ teaspoon salt
Pinch pepper
1¼ cups grated cheese
4 eggs, separated
Pinch salt for egg whites
¼ teaspoon dry mustard *or* curry powder

Place the milk in a saucepan, add the bayleaf, onion and clove and bring to the boil. Strain and cool.

Melt the butter in another saucepan, add the flour and stir until smooth, then cook for another minute without browning. Add the strained milk and stir and cook until the sauce boils and thickens. Add the tomato purée, the salt, pepper and grated cheese. Remove from the heat and add the egg yolks, beating well.

Add the salt to the egg whites and beat until peaks form, then add the dry mustard or curry powder. Fold into the tomato and cheese mixture, then place in a greased soufflé dish and bake in a moderate oven, 180° C (350° F), for 35 to 40 minutes or until puffed and brown. Serves 4.

CHEESE AND BACON SOUFFLÉ

1½ tablespoons butter
½ cup chopped bacon
2 tablespoons plain flour
¼ teaspoon dry mustard
¼ teaspoon salt
Pinch cayenne pepper
1 cup milk
1 cup grated tasty cheese
3 eggs, separated
¼ teaspoon cream of tartar

Melt the butter in a medium-sized saucepan, add the bacon, and fry lightly until the bacon fat is clear. Add the plain flour, stir until smooth then cook without browning for 3 minutes. Season with the mustard, salt and cayenne and add the milk. Stir until the sauce boils and thickens, then add the cheese and stir until it has melted. Let the sauce cool, then stir in the egg yolk.
Place the egg whites in a clean dry bowl with the cream of tartar and beat until stiff. Fold into the cheese and bacon mixture.
Pour into a well-greased soufflé dish and bake in a moderate oven, 160° C (325° F), for about 60 minutes. Serve immediately. Serves 4.

VOL-AU-VENT ST GEORGE

500 g (1 lb) puff pastry

Filling

2 level tablespoons butter
2 level tablespoons plain flour
½ level teaspoon salt
Pinch pepper
1¼ cups milk
2 cups chopped cold cooked rabbit *or* chicken *or* veal
1 set cooked brains, cut into 1 in cubes
60 g (2 oz) cooked ham, chopped
60 g (2 oz) cooked tongue, chopped
1 220 g (7 oz) can mushrooms
3 hard-boiled eggs, sliced (one for decoration)
1 teaspoon chopped parsley

Roll the pastry into an oblong shape about 1 cm (½ in) thick. Using a large oval cutter dipped in boiling water, cut out an oval shape, then with a smaller cutter cut halfway through the pastry (as you would when making small patties that are to be filled). Glaze the top lightly with egg yolk and place on a shallow oven tray. Bake in a hot oven, 230° C

(450° F), for 10 to 15 minutes. Reduce the temperature to 190° C (375° F) and bake for a further 10 minutes. Lift the centre piece of pastry and set it aside.
To make the filling, melt the butter in a saucepan, add the flour, stir until smooth, cook for 1 to 2 minutes without browning, then add the salt, pepper and milk. Stir over medium heat until the mixture boils and thickens, then stir in the chopped meats, the mushrooms, 2 sliced hard-boiled eggs and the chopped parsley. Stir gently over the heat, till piping hot.
Split the large piece of pastry through the centre and add the filling, piling it a little higher in the centre. Decorate the centre with slices of hard-boiled egg and top with the small piece of pastry that was set aside. Serves 4–6.

BACON AND MUSHROOM FLAN

3 rashers rindless bacon, chopped small
185 g (6 oz) fresh mushrooms, sliced thinly
½ bunch shallots, chopped
185 g (6 oz) short crust pastry
2 eggs
1 cup milk
¼ cup cream
Pinch cayenne pepper
1 cup shredded cheese
¼ teaspoon dry mustard

Sauté bacon, mushrooms and shallots until soft (you may require a little butter but the fat from the bacon should be sufficient). Allow to cool.
Roll the pastry and line a 20 cm (8 in) tart plate. Spread the bacon-mushroom mixture over the base. Beat the eggs and add the milk, cream, cayenne, cheese and mustard. Spoon carefully over the bacon mixture. Bake in a hot oven 230° C (450° F) for 10 minutes. Reduce the heat to moderate 180° C (350° F) and bake for a further 30 minutes or until the custard has set and the pastry lightly browned. Serve warm. Serves 6.

CAULIFLOWER AND BACON FLAN

185 g (6 oz) cheese pastry
1 medium-sized cauliflower separated into flowerlets and cooked
2 tablespoons grated cheese
½ teaspoon mustard
Pinch cayenne pepper
1½ cups white sauce
3 rashers bacon, chopped

Roll the pastry to fit a 20 cm (8 in) tart plate. Bake at 230° C (450° F) for 15 minutes. Place the drained cauliflower in the pastry case. Add the grated cheese, mustard and cayenne to the white sauce and when the cheese has melted, pour the sauce over the cauliflower.

Toss bacon in a pan over medium heat until the fat is clear. Sprinkle this over the sauce. Place in a moderate oven 180° C (350° F), to reheat before serving. Serves 6.

CAULIFLOWER AND OYSTER FLAN

185 g (6 oz) good shortcrust *or* cheese pastry
1 medium-sized cauliflower, separated into flowerlets and cooked
$1\frac{7}{8}$ cups white sauce
Squeeze lemon juice
1 egg yolk
1 dozen oysters
2 tablespoons grated cheese
1 tablespoon breadcrumbs
6 small bacon rolls

Roll the pastry to fit a 20 cm (8 in) tart plate. Bake at 230° C (450° F) for 15 minutes. Meanwhile prepare the filling. Place drained cauliflower in the cooked pastry case. Make the white sauce, adding the lemon juice and egg yolk. Stir until boiling. Beard the oysters, add to the hot sauce and pour over the cauliflower in the pie-case.
Sprinkle the top with the grated cheese and breadcrumbs and add the bacon rolls. Place in a moderate oven, 180° C (350° F), to lightly brown and melt the cheese and cook the bacon. Serve as a luncheon dish. Serves 6.

QUICHE LORRAINE

2 or 3 rashers rindless bacon, chopped
125 g (4 oz) shortcrust pastry
2 eggs
1 to $1\frac{1}{2}$ cups grated cheese
$1\frac{1}{4}$ cups milk *or* half milk and half cream
Salt
Pinch cayenne pepper
Pinch dry mustard

Garnish: 1 tomato, sliced thinly

Fry bacon lightly. Lift out and drain.
Roll the pastry thinly and line a greased 20 cm (8 in) tart plate or sandwich tin. Sprinkle with the cooked bacon.
Beat the eggs with the cheese, milk, salt to taste, cayenne and mustard. Pour over the bacon in the flan.
Bake in hot oven, 230° C (450° F), for 10 minutes. Reduce the heat to moderate, 180° C (350° F), and bake for a further 20 minutes or until the cheese custard filling has set.
Garnish the top with tomato before serving. Serves 4–6.

BACON QUICHE

Use the same method as given for Quiche Lorraine but omit the fried bacon. Instead, take rashers of bacon, remove the rind, and when the quiche has been baking for about 20 minutes, lattice the top with bacon strips and allow them to cook with the quiche.
You may prefer to garnish the baked quiche, just before serving, with strips of hot cooked bacon and slices of stuffed olives.

MUSHROOM AND ONION QUICHE

125 g (4 oz) shortcrust pastry
60 g (2 oz) butter
2 medium-sized onions, sliced
1 small can buttered mushrooms
2 eggs
$\frac{3}{4}$ cup grated cheese
Pinch dry mustard
Squeeze lemon juice
Salt
1 cup milk

Roll the pastry to line a 20 cm (8 in) tart plate or sandwich tin.
Melt the butter in a pan and lightly fry the onion until soft but not brown. Cool, then spread in the bottom of the uncooked pastry case. Cover with the mushrooms.
Beat the eggs, add the cheese, mustard, lemon juice, salt to taste, and the milk. Pour carefully over the mushroom mixture in the uncooked pastry case. Bake in a hot oven, 220° C (425° F), for 10 minutes, then reduce the heat to moderate, 180° C (350° F), and continue baking for a further 20 minutes or until the custard has set and the pastry is lightly browned. Serves 6.

SALMON AND ASPARAGUS QUICHE

1 quantity cheese pastry
1 212 g ($7\frac{1}{2}$ g) can salmon
2 tablespoons chopped shallot
1 439 g ($15\frac{1}{2}$ oz) can asparagus cuts
Milk *or* half milk, half cream
2 eggs
Salt and pepper
1 tablespoon grated cheese

Cheese pastry
$1\frac{1}{2}$ cups plain flour
$\frac{1}{2}$ level teaspoon baking powder
$\frac{1}{4}$ teaspoon salt
Pinch cayenne pepper
$\frac{1}{4}$ teaspoon mustard
90 g (3 oz) butter
60 g (2 oz) cheese, grated
1 egg yolk
2 tablespoons cold water
Lemon juice

Sift together the dry ingredients for the pastry then rub in the butter and add the grated cheese. Beat the egg yolk with the water, a good squeeze lemon juice and use to mix the dry ingredients into a fairly firm dough.

Turn it on to a lightly floured board and knead only until smooth on the outside. Roll to line a 23 cm (9 in) flan ring, trimming the edges neatly. Drain the salmon, reserving the liquid, then flake the flesh lightly and spread it evenly in the bottom of the uncooked pastry shell. Sprinkle with chopped shallots and then with the well drained asparagus pieces. Add enough milk to the drained salmon liquid to make one cup and stir into the lightly beaten eggs. Season with salt and pepper and carefully pour over the ingredients in the pastry shell. Sprinkle with the grated cheese. Bake in a hot oven 230° C (450° F) for 10 minutes, reduce the heat to 180° C (350° F) and cook for a further 30 minutes or until the custard filling has set and the pastry lightly browned. Serves 6.

SEAFOOD QUICHE

125–185 g (4 to 6 oz) shortcrust pastry
Egg white
125 g ($\frac{1}{4}$ lb) cooked *or* canned crabmeat *or* prawns *or* crayfish, shredded
2 tablespoons chopped spring onions
$\frac{1}{2}$ cup coarsely grated Swiss *or* Cheddar cheese
2 eggs
$\frac{2}{3}$ cup milk
1 tablespoon tomato paste
$\frac{1}{2}$ teaspoon salt
$\frac{1}{4}$ teaspoon pepper

Line a 20 cm (8 in) flan tin or pie plate with the pastry. Brush the surface with egg white. Spread the seafood over the pastry, then sprinkle with the spring onion and half the cheese.

Beat together the eggs, milk, tomato paste, salt and pepper. Pour over the seafood and onions and sprinkle with the remaining cheese.

Bake in a hot oven, 220° C (425° F), for 10 minutes. Reduce the heat to 180° C (350° F) and bake for a further 30 to 35 minutes or until the custard has set and the top is a golden colour. Serves 6.

ASPARAGUS AND CHICKEN PIE

185 g (6 oz) shortcrust pastry
1 small can asparagus spears
1$\frac{1}{4}$ cups diced cooked chicken
3 slices bacon, fried and crumbled
$\frac{1}{2}$ cup shredded cheese
1 tablespoon Parmesan cheese
2 eggs
2 teaspoons plain flour
1 cup milk
$\frac{1}{2}$ teaspoon salt
$\frac{1}{4}$ teaspoon nutmeg
$\frac{1}{4}$ teaspoon cayenne pepper

Roll the pastry and cut to fit a 23 cm (9 in) tart plate.

Drain the liquid from the asparagus spears. Mix the chopped chicken, bacon and cheese and spread in the bottom of the uncooked pastry case.

Beat the eggs slightly, then beat in the flour, milk, salt, nutmeg and cayenne. Pour carefully over the mixture in the pastry shell. Arrange the well-drained asparagus spears on top in a spoke design.

Bake in a hot oven, 200° C (400° F), for 10 minutes, then reduce the heat to 180° C (350° F) and bake for another 40 to 45 minutes or until the custard has set. Serves 6.

CRAB AND LEEK PIE

180 g (6 oz) short crust pastry
1 cup shredded cheese
2 tender leeks
1 tablespoon butter
1 170 g (5$\frac{1}{2}$ oz) can crabmeat, well drained
3 eggs
$\frac{3}{4}$ cup milk
$\frac{1}{2}$ cup cream
$\frac{1}{4}$ teaspoon dry mustard
1 teaspoon lemon juice
Rind of 1 lemon, grated
Pinch nutmeg

Line a 20 or 23 cm (8 or 9 in) pie plate with the pastry and brush the surface with a little unbeaten egg white (you can use a little of the eggs intended for the filling). Prick the bottom of the pastry lightly to prevent it rising in the centre and then sprinkle with half the cheese.

Split the leeks lengthwise, wash thoroughly, discard the coarse green leaves and chop the remaining tender stalks. Sauté them in butter until limp then add the crabmeat. Mix lightly before spreading over the cheese in the pastry shell.

In a bowl beat the eggs lightly and add the milk, cream, mustard, lemon rind and juice and the nutmeg. Pour carefully over the crab mixture then sprinkle with the remaining cheese.

Bake in a hot oven 220° C (425° F) for 10 minutes then reduce the heat to moderate 160° C (325° F) for a further 30 to 40 minutes or until the custard has set and the pastry lightly browned. Serve hot or warm. Serves 6.

TOMATO CHEESE PIE

185 g (6 oz) shortcrust pastry
1 medium-sized firm tomato
3 eggs
1$\frac{1}{4}$ cups milk
$\frac{1}{2}$ teaspoon salt
$\frac{1}{4}$ teaspoon pepper
$\frac{1}{4}$ cup finely chopped parsley
125 g (4 oz) Cheddar cheese, grated
6 slices bacon, crisped and crumbled

Used it. Brian liked + 2 pie crusts + 1 lb tomatoes

Roll the pastry thinly and use to line a 20 cm (8 in) tart plate. Flute or pinch the edges. Cut the tomato into eight wedges and arrange on the bottom of the uncooked pastry case.

Beat the eggs with the milk, salt, pepper and chopped parsley, and sprinkle in the grated cheese and crumbled bacon. Pour this over the tomato wedges.

Bake in a hot oven 230° C (450° F) for 10 minutes. Reduce the temperature to 160° C (325° F) and bake for another 30 to 35 minutes or until the custard has set and is lightly browned. Let stand for 10 minutes, then cut into wedges to serve. Serves 6.

ITALIAN CHEESE PIE

185 g (6 oz) shortcrust pastry
4 good-sized tomatoes
2 125 g (4 oz) cans sardines
2 cups grated cheese
1 tablespoon chopped onion
Salt and pepper
2 teaspoons finely chopped parsley
8 stuffed olives, sliced
2 teaspoons Worcestershire sauce
1 rounded tablespoon plain flour

Roll the pastry to line a 20 cm (8 in) tart plate. Prick the bottom to prevent rising, and pinch a frill round the edge. Bake in a hot oven, 200° C (400° F) for 10 to 12 minutes.

While the pastry shell is cooking, cut two of the tomatoes into thin slices and the other two into slices about $\frac{1}{4}$ inch thick. Reserve the thin slices for topping the pie.

Drain the oil from the sardines and arrange them in the cooked pastry shell. Cover with a layer of grated cheese, add the onion, salt and pepper to taste, the parsley, the olives and the thick slices of tomato. Sprinkle with the Worcestershire sauce, add another layer of grated cheese, then dust lightly with the plain flour.

Arrange the thin slices of tomato in the form of petals on top of the pie. Place in a slow oven for about 20 minutes to heat and cook the filling. Serves 6.

ITALIAN SPINACH PIE

125 g–185 g (4–6 oz) short crust pastry
250 g ($\frac{1}{2}$ lb) frozen spinach
2 rashers bacon, chopped small
125 g (4 oz) cream cheese
2 eggs
$\frac{1}{2}$ cup cream
$\frac{1}{2}$ cup milk
Salt and black pepper, freshly ground
Pinch nutmeg

Line a greased 20 cm (8 in) flan ring or tart plate with the pastry. Remove the rind and chop the bacon into small pieces. Fry until crisp. Drain and cool. Cook the spinach according to the directions on the packet. Drain thoroughly, add the cream cheese and allow to cool. Stir in the bacon.

Beat the eggs lightly and add the milk, cream, black pepper and nutmeg. Season to taste with a little salt. Spread the cheese and spinach mixture over the base of the uncooked pastry then carefully cover with the egg mixture.

Bake in a hot oven 220° C (425° F) for 10 minutes. Reduce the heat to 180° C (350° F) and cook for a further 30 to 35 minutes or until the custard has set and the top lightly browned. Serves 6.

BACON AND TOMATO PIZZA

Pizza crust

60 g (2 oz) plain flour
60 g (2 oz) self-raising flour
$\frac{1}{4}$ teaspoon salt
$\frac{1}{4}$ level teaspoon dry mustard
Pinch cayenne pepper
30 g (1 oz) butter *or* margarine
1 egg
2 tablespoons milk

Filling

250 g ($\frac{1}{2}$ lb) bacon rashers
2 cups onion, sliced
3 tomatoes, peeled and sliced thickly
1 teaspoon oregano
$\frac{1}{2}$ teaspoon salt
$\frac{1}{4}$ teaspoon pepper
250 g (8 oz) Mozzarella cheese, sliced
$\frac{1}{4}$ cup stuffed olives, sliced

Sift the flours into a bowl with the salt, mustard and cayenne. Rub in the butter or margarine.

Beat the egg with the milk and use to mix the dry ingredients into a rather firm dough. Turn on to a floured board and knead only until smooth on the outside. Roll out 3 mm ($\frac{1}{8}$ in) thick and use to line a pizza plate, pressing the dough neatly into the form of the plate.

Sauté the bacon lightly in a pan and drain it, reserving about 2 tablespoons of the bacon fat. In this fat sauté the onion slices until tender.

Peel the tomatoes and cut into 5 mm ($\frac{1}{4}$ in) thick slices. Arrange these in a single layer in the uncooked pizza shell, spread over them the sautéed onion and sprinkle with the oregano, salt and pepper. Cover with the bacon rashers and arrange slices of cheese and stuffed olive over all.

Bake at 190° C (375° F) for 20 to 25 minutes or until the crust is cooked and the cheese melted and lightly browned. Serve piping hot cut into wedges. Serves 6.

BURGER PIZZA

1 unbaked pizza crust (see bacon and tomato pizza, p.   )
1 tablespoon butter
1 tablespoon oil
250 g (½ lb) finely minced steak
1 large onion, chopped
1 clove garlic, crushed
1 tablespoon chopped celery
1 tablespoon chopped parsley
3 medium tomatoes, sliced
60 g (2 oz) salami, sliced thinly
125 g (4 oz) sharp cheese, sliced thinly

Prepare the pizza crust and dot with pieces of butter.
Heat the oil in a pan and lightly sauté the minced steak until it changes colour. Turn on to a plate and allow to cool.
Combine chopped onion, crushed garlic, and chopped celery and parsley. Spread the minced steak over the uncooked pastry and sprinkle the onion mixture over it. Arrange over-lapping tomato slices and salami on top, then add slices of cheese.
Bake at 190° C (375° F) for about 25 minutes or until the filling is cooked and the pastry nicely browned. Serves 6.

MEATBALL AND MOZZARELLA PIZZA

500 g (1 lb) finely minced steak
¼ cup dry breadcrumbs
2 tablespoons minced onion
1 egg
1 teaspoon salt
¼ teaspoon pepper
½ teaspoon oregano
1½ tablespoons olive oil
1½ cups tomato sauce (see below)
250 g (8 oz) Mozzarella cheese, grated
1 unbaked pizza case (see bacon and tomato pizza p. 52)

Combine the minced steak with the breadcrumbs, onion, beaten egg, salt, pepper and oregano, mixing until well blended. Shape portions into 1 in balls, then flatten each with the palm of the hand.
Heat the oil in a pan and brown the meatballs on all sides. This will take about 10 minutes. Drain well.
Spread the tomato sauce over the unbaked pizza case, cover with the meatballs and sprinkle with the cheese.
Bake at 190° C (375° F) for 20 to 25 minutes or until the pizza case is cooked and the cheese melted and lightly browned. Cut into wedges and serve piping hot. Serves 6.

Tomato sauce

1½ tablespoons oil
1 cup onion, sliced
1 clove garlic, crushed
470 g (15 oz) can undrained tomatoes
2 teaspoons chopped parsley
1½ teaspoons salt
1 teaspoon oregano
½ teaspoon sugar
¼ teaspoon basil
¼ teaspoon black pepper

TOMATO SAUCE

Heat the oil in a medium-sized saucepan and sauté the sliced onion and crushed garlic until the onion is golden.
Add the tomatoes, parsley, salt, oregano, sugar, basil and pepper. Bring to the boil. Reduce the heat, then simmer uncovered for 45 minutes, stirring occasionally. Remove from the heat and allow to cool before using in the pizza fillings.

PIZZA MILANO

1 unbaked pizza crust (see bacon and tomato pizza)
2 teaspoons butter
1 tablespoon olive oil
250 g (½ lb) finely minced steak
3 medium-sized tomatoes, coarsely chopped
4 tablespoons anchovies, chopped finely (optional)
1 large onion, chopped finely
1 clove garlic, crushed
1 tablespoon chopped celery
1 tablespoon chopped parsley
125 g (¼ lb) good sharp cheese, grated

Prepare the pizza crust and dot with pieces of butter.
Heat the oil in a pan and lightly sauté the minced steak until it changes colour. Turn out on to a plate and allow to cool.
Peel and coarsely chop the tomatoes and combine with the anchovies, finely chopped onion, crushed garlic, chopped celery and parsley, grated cheese and cooked meat. Spread this mixture over the unbaked pizza crust and bake in a moderate oven, 190° C (375° F), for 20 to 25 minutes or until the filling is cooked and the crust brown. Serves 6.

SALAMI AND GREEN PEPPER PIZZA

1½ cups tomato sauce (see meatball and Mozzarella
  pizza p. 53)
1 unbaked pizza crust (see bacon and tomato pizza p. 52)
125 g (¼ lb) salami
½ cup onion rings
½ cup green pepper rings
250 g (8 oz) Mozzarella cheese, sliced

Spread the tomato sauce over the unbaked pizza crust and arrange salami slices, onion rings and green pepper rings on top. Cover with sliced cheese.
Bake at 190° C (375° F) for 20 to 25 minutes or until the crust is cooked and the cheese melted and lightly browned. Serve piping hot. Serves 6.

SPAGHETTI BOLOGNESE

90 g (3 oz) butter
1 onion, sliced
2 rashers streaky bacon, chopped
1 carrot, diced
1 stalk celery, chopped
125 g (4 oz) finely minced steak
60 g (2 oz) chicken livers, washed and cleaned
2 teaspoons tomato paste
¾ cup white wine
1¼ cups stock *or* water and a soup cube
Salt and pepper
1 clove garlic, crushed
375 g (12 oz) spaghetti
125 g (4 oz) cheese, grated

Melt 30 g (1 oz) of the butter, add onion and sauté until soft but not brown. Add bacon, carrot and celery, and cook and stir until lightly browned. Add the minced meat and stir over the heat until all of it is moistened, then add the chicken livers, stirring and cooking till moistened also. Add the tomato paste, wine and stock, season with salt and pepper, then add crushed garlic. Cover and simmer gently for 40 minutes or until the sauce is thick and the meat very tender.
Cook the spaghetti in the usual way. Drain, then stir in one-third of the meat sauce and the remaining 60 g (2 oz) of butter. Place in a hot serving dish, pour over the remainder of the sauce and sprinkle with grated cheese. Serves 4.

SPAGHETTI MARINARA

500 g (1 lb) spaghetti
1 large onion, sliced
2 cloves garlic, crushed
2 tablespoons oil
500 g (1 lb) ripe tomatoes, peeled, seeded and chopped
Salt and black pepper, freshly ground
1 teaspoon brown sugar
½ teaspoon oregano *or* marjoram
500 g (1 lb) prawns
5 tablespoons dry white wine
2 tablespoons chopped parsley
Butter

Sauté the onion and garlic in the oil until the onion is transparent. Add tomatoes to the saucepan together with the salt, pepper, sugar and oregano or marjoram. Cover and simmer for about 15 minutes.
Shell and devein the prawns, chop them if they are king size and place in a small saucepan with the wine. Cover and simmer for five minutes.
Rub the tomato mixture through a sieve, reheat in a saucepan then add the prawns and parsley. Taste and add more salt and pepper if necessary.

While the sauce is simmering cook the spaghetti in boiling salted water for about 12 minutes. Drain, add a generous knob of butter and sauté for a few minutes. Place in a hot serving dish and pour over the prawn sauce. Serves 6.

MACARONI CHEESE

1 rounded tablespoon butter
2 rounded tablespoons plain flour
¼ teaspoon salt
Pinch cayenne pepper
½ level teaspoon mustard
2 cups milk
1 cup cooked macaroni
¾ cup cheese, grated
1 tablespoon soft white breadcrumbs

Melt the butter in a saucepan and add the flour, salt, cayenne and mustard. Stir until smooth, then cook for 1 minute over medium heat. Do not allow to brown.
Add the milk and stir until the sauce boils and thickens. Stir in the cooked macaroni and half the grated cheese.
Place in a greased casserole and sprinkle the remainder of the cheese and the breadcrumbs on top. Bake in a moderate oven until the sauce bubbles and the cheese melts and lightly browns. Serves 4.

MACARONI SUPPER RAMEKINS

250 g (½ lb) macaroni
1 tablespoon butter
1 tablespoon onion, minced finely
2 tablespoons plain flour
½ teaspoon salt
Pinch pepper
1 teaspoon mustard
2 cups milk
1 cup cheese, grated
1 cup cooked peas
½ teaspoon Worcestershire sauce
2 hard-boiled eggs
2 tomatoes, sliced thickly

Cook the macaroni in plenty of boiling salted water for 15 minutes, then drain. Melt the butter in a sauce-pan and sauté the onion until soft but not brown. Add the plain flour, salt, pepper and mustard. Cook for 1 minute. Add the milk and continue to cook, stirring well, until the sauce boils and thickens.
Remove the sauce from the heat and add the maca-roni and half the grated cheese. If peas are used, add them at this stage. Flavour with the Worcestershire sauce. Shell and quarter the eggs and add to the mixture.
Divide evenly between six well-greased ramekins and top each with a thick slice of tomato and a sprinkling of the remaining cheese. Bake in a moder-ate oven, 180° C (350° F), until the cheese melts and browns and the tomato softens. Serves 6.

LASAGNE

500 g (1 lb) minced beef
1 tablespoon oil
1 clove garlic, peeled and crushed
2 teaspoons parsley, chopped
½ teaspoon oregano
1 teaspoon salt
1 large can peeled tomatoes
1 125 g (4 oz) can tomato paste
⅛ teaspoon pepper
250 g (½ lb) lasagne noodles
250 g (½ lb) Mozzarella cheese, thinly sliced
750 g (¾ lb) cream style cottage cheese
2 tablespoons grated Parmesan cheese

Brown the beef in the oil and add the garlic, parsley, oregano and salt. Let the beef stand for about 10 minutes then spoon off any excess fat. Add the tomatoes, tomato paste and pepper. Stir until boiling then lower the heat, cover and simmer for one hour. Towards the end of the cooking time remove the lid and increase the heat slightly in order to evapo-rate some of the liquid.
Cook the noodles in boiling salted water for about 15 minutes. Drain well. In the bottom of a greased casserole place one third of the noodles then top with one third of the cottage cheese, half the Mozzarella cheese and half the meat sauce. Add another third of the noodles, then the remainder of the cottage cheese covered with the remainder of the Mozzarella. Add the rest of the noodles and the rest of the meat sauce. Sprinkle with the Parmesan cheese and bake in a moderate oven for about 20 or 30 minutes or until the contents of the casserole bubbles and is thoroughly heated through. Serves 6.

RISOTTO PROVENÇAL

Risotto
2 tablespoons olive oil
1 large onion, chopped
125 g (½ lb) raw rice
Hot water
Salt and pepper

Sauce
2 tablespoons onion, chopped finely
1 tablespoon olive oil
¼ pint dry white wine
4 tomatoes
Salt and pepper
1 clove of garlic, crushed
2 tablespoons chopped parsley
¼ teaspoon saffron powder
½ green pepper, chopped finely

Heat the oil for the risotto in a pan and sauté the onion until golden. Add the rice and cook, stirring constantly, until it is golden. Moisten with 1¼ cups of hot water and simmer gently, stirring occasionally and adding more hot water as required and as the liquid is absorbed by the rice. Continue cooking until the rice is soft but not mushy. Season to taste with salt and pepper.
To make the sauce, sauté the 2 tablespoons onion in the oil until tender, then stir in the wine. Add peeled and coarsely chopped tomatoes. Season with salt and pepper, then add garlic, parsley and saffron. Simmer gently for 20 minutes, then add green pep-per and simmer for a further 15 minutes. Serves 4.

RISOTTO WITH SAUSAGEBURGERS

½ cup raw rice
1 tablespoon butter
2 cups chicken broth *or* water and a chicken soup cube
¼ cup cheese, grated
Pinch cayenne pepper
Pinch paprika
Pinch saffron
1 teaspoon salt
1 small clove garlic, crushed (optional)

Sauté the raw rice in the butter until a straw colour. Pour the heated broth over it, then add the cheese, cayenne, paprika, saffron, salt and the garlic if used. Steam in the top of a double saucepan for about 30 minutes or until the rice is tender but not mushy, stirring occasionally to prevent sticking. Serve topped with sausageburgers. Serves 4.

SAUSAGEBURGERS

500 g (1 lb) finely minced steak
125 g (¼ lb) Italian sausage, finely chopped or minced
1 egg, slightly beaten
1 cup soft white breadcrumbs
½ cup milk
1 clove garlic, crushed
1 small onion, chopped
1 teaspoon salt
1 tablespoon butter
1 tablespoon oil

Mix the minced steak, finely chopped or minced sausage and slightly beaten egg. Soak the breadcrumbs in the milk, squeeze dry and combine with the meat. Sauté garlic and onion in the butter with the salt. Add this to the meat mixture, then form into tiny balls and brown quickly in hot oil. Cover and cook for about 5 minutes.

ITALIAN RISOTTO WITH HAM

125 g (4 oz) butter
1 onion, chopped
1½ cups raw rice
2½ cups consommé or chicken stock
1 cup water
2 teaspoons salt
Pinch pepper
1 cup diced ham
Parmesan cheese, grated

Heat the butter in a pan, add onion and sauté until soft. Add the rice and cook to a straw colour, stirring constantly. Add enough hot consommé and water to just cover the rice, stir well and continue to cook, adding more water or stock as needed and stirring to prevent sticking and burning.
When the rice is a little more than half done, add the salt, pepper and ham. Continue cooking, adding more liquid as required and continuing to stir.
When the rice is soft and most of the liquid has been absorbed, take off the heat and turn the rice into a dish. Sprinkle with the cheese just before serving. Serves 6.

LOBSTER CRÉME RISOTTO

3 tablespoons butter
2 tablespoons chopped shallot
2 tablespoons plain flour
2 teaspoons curry powder
1¼ cups milk
½ cup cream
¼ teaspoon salt
Pinch pepper
1 egg yolk
2 teaspoons tomato paste
1½ cups chopped lobster meat
¾ cup rice
Salt
Chicken stock or water and stock cube

Garnish: lemon and parsley

Melt 2 tablespoons butter in a saucepan and add the shallots. Sauté until soft but not brown. Add the flour and curry powder and stir until smooth then cook without browning for one or two minutes. Season with salt and pepper and then add the milk and cream. Stir over a medium heat until the sauce boils and thickens.
Add egg yolk, tomato paste and lobster meat and stir until smooth. Keep hot over boiling water while you cook the rice.
Melt remaining butter in a saucepan and add the rice. Toss until the grains are coated. Now add salt to taste, enough stock or water to cover and reach about halfway up the saucepan. Bring to the boil and cook until the grains are tender. Drain, run some hot water through while the rice is still in the colander, then drain again and pack into a ring mould.
Unmould the ring on to a hot serving dish and fill the centre with the curried lobster. Serve with a lemon and parsley garnish. Serves 4–6.

FRIED RICE BAMBOO

1½ cups raw rice
250 g (½ lb) pork fillets
1 slightly rounded teaspoon cornflour
Pinch salt
Pinch pepper
1 teaspoon sugar
2 teaspoons soy sauce
2 tablespoons lard or peanut oil
½ bunch spring onions, diced
250 g (½ lb) firm cooked peas
1 egg beaten with ¼ cup milk

The day before the dish of fried rice is to be made, wash the rice thoroughly and cook in plenty of boiling salted water. Drain, rinse and spread to dry. Slice the pork into very thin strips and place in a bowl with the cornflour, salt, pepper, sugar and soy sauce, mixing to make sure each piece of pork is coated.

Italian Spinach Pie (p. 52).

Spaghetti Marinara (p. 54).

Heat the oil in a pan until it is smoking. Add the pork pieces and sauté over high heat, turning the meat frequently until it is browned on all sides. Remove from the pan and chop into small pieces. Return the frying pan to the heat, add a little more oil and lightly fry the onions and the peas. Add the minced pork and the cooked rice, mixing well together. Heat thoroughly over low heat.

Season egg and milk mixture with salt and pepper, fry in a small pan, making a thin, flat omelette. Chop and add to the rice in the pan. Reheat thoroughly, adjusting the seasonings and using a little more soy sauce if liked, or serve with soy sauce. Serves 6.

CURRIED EGGS WITH RICE

3 cups cooked rice
1 dozen small eggs
60 g (2 oz) butter
$\frac{1}{2}$ cup chopped onion
$\frac{1}{2}$ cup chopped apple
60 g (2 oz) plain flour
3 teaspoons curry powder
3 cups milk
1 teaspoon salt
1 teaspoon sugar
1 teaspoon lemon juice
$\frac{1}{2}$–$\frac{3}{4}$ teaspoon Worcestershire sauce (optional)

Garnish: lemon wedges and parsley

Place the eggs in a saucepan, cover with cold water, bring to the boil and simmer for 10 minutes. Remove from the heat, crack the shells and immediately place them in cold water to prevent the yolks from discolouring.

Melt the butter in a saucepan, add the apple and onion and sauté until both are soft. Blend in the flour and curry powder. Cook for two or three minutes then add the milk and stir until the sauce boils and thickens. Season to taste with the salt, sugar, lemon juice and, if liked, the Worcestershire sauce. Simmer for about 10 minutes.

Meanwhile, shell the eggs and cut them in halves lengthwise. Fold them carefully into the curry sauce and reheat. Have the rice freshly cooked and well drained. Turn it into the serving dish and spoon over the curried eggs. Serve with lemon wedges and a parsley garnish. Serves 6.

STUFFED FISH FILLETS

6 fish fillets
$\frac{1}{4}$ teaspoon pepper
1 teaspoon salt
Lemon juice
1 tablespoon butter
2 small onions, peeled and chopped
250 g ($\frac{1}{2}$ lb) mushrooms, sliced
1 tablespoon chopped parsley
250 g ($\frac{1}{2}$ lb) cooked prawns
2 tablespoons plain flour
1 cup cream *or* $\frac{1}{2}$ cup milk and $\frac{1}{2}$ cup cream
$\frac{1}{2}$ cup white wine
1 tablespoon cognac (optional)
$\frac{1}{2}$ cup grated cheese

Garnish: lemon wedges and parsley

Sprinkle the fish fillets with pepper, salt and lemon juice and set aside. Melt the butter in a saucepan and add the onions and mushrooms. Sauté until the onion is golden and the mushroom soft. Stir in the parsley and prawns. Place a spoonful of this mixture on each fillet, roll it up and secure with wooden toothpicks. Arrange them side by side in a shallow, lightly greased casserole.

To the remaining mushroom mixture (you will only have used about half the quantity) add the flour and cook for one or two minutes without browning then add the cream, wine and cognac, if used, and stir until boiling.

Pour over the fish in the casserole and sprinkle with the cheese. Bake in a moderate oven for 20 to 25 minutes or until the cheese melts and browns, the sauce bubbles and the fish flakes when tested with a fork. Serve with lemon wedges and parsley garnish. Serves 6.

SALMON AND ASPARAGUS CHANTILLY

440 g (14 oz) canned salmon
Milk
2 tablespoons butter
2 teaspoons grated or finely chopped onion *or* shallot
2 slightly rounded tablespoons plain flour
2 teaspoons chopped parsley
1 teaspoon prepared mustard
1 tablespoon mayonnaise
1 level teaspoon salt
Pepper
3 hard-boiled eggs, sliced
1 340 g (11 oz) can asparagus spears
2 tablespoons soft white breadcrumbs
2 tablespoons grated cheese

Garnish: lemon wedges and parsley

Drain the liquid from the salmon, remove the skin and bones and flake the flesh lightly. Measure the salmon liquid and make up to 2 cups with milk. Melt the butter in a saucepan, add the onion or shallot and sauté until soft but not brown. Stir in the flour and cook for 1 minute, then add the milk. Cook, stirring constantly until the sauce boils and thickens, then remove from the heat and add the parsley, mustard, mayonnaise, salt and pepper.

Place a layer of the sauce in a lightly greased casserole, then add alternate layers of salmon, sliced egg and asparagus. Cover with the remainder of the sauce, and sprinkle the top with the combined breadcrumbs and cheese.

Bake in a moderate oven, 180° C (350° F), for about 30 minutes or until the top is lightly browned. Serve garnished with lemon wedges and parsley. Serves 6.

QUICK SALMON RISSOLES

1 cup cold water
3 tablespoons instant mashed potato
2 tablespoons chopped shallots
1 250 g (8 oz) canned salmon
Lemon juice
Seasoned flour
Butter for cooking

Garnish: lemon wedges

Bring the water to the boil, add the instant mashed potato and stir with a fork until fluffy. Drain and flake the salmon and mix with the potatoes then add the shallots and flavour with a good squeeze lemon juice.

Divide the mixture into eight equal portions. Shape them into round flat cakes in seasoned flour.

Heat about a tablespoon of butter in a 20 cm (8 in) frying pan (or enough to coat the surface of the pan). When it is sizzling add the rissoles and cook fairly quickly until brown on one side. Use an egg slicer to turn the rissoles and cook on the other side. Lift out and serve at once. Successful cooking with these rissoles depends on the small amount of butter used in the pan and the quickness with which they are fried to make the surface crisp and the centre firm. If too much butter is used and the cooking is slow the rissoles will soak up the butter and become greasy and badly shaped. Serve with lemon wedges. Serves 4.

CURRIED FISH CAKES

1 rounded teaspoon butter
1 teaspoon finely chopped shallot
1 slightly rounded teaspoon curry powder
250 g (8 oz) salmon
1 lemon
1 teaspoon lemon juice
2 cups freshly cooked mashed potato
Salt and pepper
1 egg
Seasoned flour
Breadcrumbs
Hot oil or fat

Garnish: lemon slices and parsley sprigs

Melt the butter in a saucepan and add the shallots. Cook until soft but not brown. Add the curry powder and cook for a few minutes longer. Add the drained and flaked salmon, the lemon rind and juice and the mashed potato.

Season with salt and pepper and bind with a little of the eaten egg. Mix the remainder of the egg with a little milk and use for glazing.

Turn the mixture on to a plate to cool. Take tablespoonful and shape into round flat cakes in seasoned flour. Dip one at a time in the egg glazing then cover with the breadcrumbs.

Deep fry in hot fat or oil until a golden brown. Drain on absorbent paper and serve with a lemon and parsley garnish. Serves 4.

FISH PORTUGUESE

4 fillets white fleshed fish
Bouquet garni or 3 mixed herb cubes
2 tablespoons oil
1 onion, peeled and chopped
2 medium tomatoes, peeled and chopped
1 cup celery, sliced
½ cup dry white wine

Garnish: lemon and parsley

Place the fish in a lightly greased casserole and sprinkle with the herbs or add the bouquet garni. Heat the oil, add the onions and cook until they begin to brown then add the tomatoes and celery and continue cooking for a few minutes. Add the wine, stir until boiling then pour the vegetable mixture over the fish. Cover and bake in a moderate oven 180° C (350° F) for about 30 minutes. Serve with a lemon and parsley garnish. Serves 4.

FISH PARMENTIER

4 fish fillets
Lemon juice
Seasoned flour
Butter for frying
125 g (4 oz) instant potato
Mayonnaise
⅓ cup chopped shallot
Salt and pepper
Cheese, grated

Garnish: lemon and parsley

Sprinkle the fish fillets with lemon juice then coat them with seasoned flour. Heat a little butter in a pan and fry the fish lightly on both sides. Meanwhile prepare the instant potato as directed on the packet and flavour with a little mayonnaise before stirring in the shallots. Season to taste with salt and pepper.

Top each fish fillet thickly with the potato and sprinkle with cheese. Grill or bake in a moderate oven until the cheese melts and browns. Garnish with lemon and parsley. Serves 4.

TURBANS OF WHITING WITH ORANGE CAPER SAUCE

8 medium whiting fillets
3 tablespoons butter
2 teaspoons grated orange rind
½ teaspoon salt
¼ teaspoon pepper
2 tablespoons seasoned flour
1 egg
½ cup milk
Soft white breadcrumbs
Oil *or* fat

Sauce

½ cup cooked salad dressing
½ cup cream *or* canned, evaporated milk
2 tablespoons orange juice
1 teaspoon lemon juice
2 teaspoons grated orange rind
1 tablespoon chopped capers
1 teaspoon finely chopped parsley
1 tablespoon finely chopped shallot

Brush each fillet with the melted butter and sprinkle with the grated orange rind, salt and pepper. Roll each fillet into a turban shape beginning at the tail, and fasten with a wooden toothpick. Cover each in seasoned flour then dip in a mixture of the beaten egg and milk before coating with breadcrumbs.
Deep fry the fish in hot fat or oil until they are golden in colour. Drain on paper, remove the wooden toothpicks and serve immediately with the orange caper sauce.
To make the sauce, combine all ingredients in the order given and chill until serving time. Serves 4–8.

LITTLE CHICKEN RAMEKINS

2 medium-sized carrots
2 medium-sized potatoes
2½ cups white sauce
1 teaspoon chopped parsley
3 cups chopped cooked chicken
½ cup chopped celery
2 tablespoons minced onion
2 tablespoons chopped cooked bacon *or* ham
1 220 g (7 oz) can buttered mushrooms
125 g (4 oz) shortcrust pastry *or* 1 pound fluffy mashed potato

Cook the carrots and potatoes until almost tender. Drain and cut into 1 cm (½ in) pieces. Divide evenly between six greased ramekins.
Make the white sauce and add the parsley, chicken, celery, onion, bacon or ham and mushrooms. Spoon this over the vegetables in the ramekins.
Roll the pastry thinly and cut into six rounds large enough to cover the top of each ramekin. Tuck the pastry inside the rim of the ramekin, make a slit or

two in the top to allow the steam to escape, and bake in a hot oven, 220° C (425° F), for about 20 minutes.
Instead of the pastry, fluffy mashed potato could be spread or piped on top—in this case bake in a moderate oven, 180° C (350° F), until the sauce mixture bubbles and the potato topping is a light brown. Serves 6.

MARYLAND CROQUETTES

3 cups chopped cooked chicken
½ cup chopped cooked bacon *or* ham
1 tablespoon chopped parsley
1 tablespoon butter
2 slightly rounded tablespoons plain flour
1 teaspoon salt
¼ teaspoon pepper
½ teaspoon dry mustard
1½ cups milk
2 hard-boiled eggs, chopped
Seasoned flour
1 egg, beaten with a little milk
Breadcrumbs
Oil *or* fat

Mix the chicken with the bacon and parsley. Melt the butter in a small saucepan, add the flour, stir until smooth then cook for about two minutes without browning. Season with the salt, pepper and mustard and add the milk. Cook, stirring constantly until the sauce boils and thickens.
Add the meat mixture and the chopped hard boiled egg and turn out on a plate to cool.
Take spoonsful of the mixture and make into cork shapes in the seasoned flour. Dip each one in egg mixture then coat with breadcrumbs. Deep fry until a golden brown. Drain on paper and serve with fried bananas and creamed corn in lettuce cups. Serves 6–8.

CHICKEN RICE CROQUETTES

60 g (2 oz) butter
60 g (2 oz) plain flour
1¼ cups milk
½ teaspoon salt
¼ teaspoon pepper
1 cup cooked rice
2 cups finely chopped, cooked chicken
1 tablespoon finely chopped onion *or* shallot
1 tablespoon chopped parsley
Salt and pepper
2 tablespoons flour
1 egg, beaten with a little milk
Soft white breadcrumbs
Oil *or* fat

Garnish: parsley sprigs

Melt the butter in a saucepan and add the flour, cook one minute without browning then add the milk and stir until the sauce boils and thickens. Season to taste with salt and pepper. Continue to cook for two or three minutes then stir in the rice, chicken, shallot and parsley. Mix thoroughly, turn out on to a plate and allow to cool.

Mix the salt and pepper with the flour. Beat the egg with a little milk to make the glazing. Take spoonsful of the mixture and shape into cork shapes in the seasoned flour. Dip each one in egg mixture then coat with breadcrumbs. Chill for at least half an hour if time permits.

Deep fry the croquettes in hot fat until a golden brown, drain on paper and serve hot with a parsley garnish. Serves 6–8.

CHICKEN CRUNCH

¾ cup uncooked rice
1 medium-sized onion, chopped
1 tablespoon butter
1 medium-sized green pepper, chopped
3 cups diced celery
1¼ cups chicken stock
2 teaspoons soy sauce
2 cups diced cooked chicken
1 220 g (7 oz) can buttered mushrooms
Salt and pepper
1 tablespoon cornflour
½ cup slivered almonds
Freshly boiled rice

Cook the rice in plenty of boiling salted water. Sauté onion in the butter until tender. Stir in green pepper, celery, chicken stock and soy sauce.

Simmer for 10 minutes, then add the chicken and mushrooms. Season to taste with salt and pepper. Blend the cornflour with a little cold water and stir into the chicken mixture. Cook, stirring well until the mixture returns to the boil. Add the nuts. Serve over freshly cooked rice. Serves 6.

CHICKEN LIVER SAUTÉ

250 g (½ lb) bacon rashers
375 g (¾ lb) chicken livers, washed and cleaned
Seasoned flour
1 cup stock or water and soup cube
1 220 g (7 oz) can buttered mushrooms
1 tablespoon soy sauce
2 tablespoons sherry
Salt and pepper
Hot buttered toast

Garnish: parsley sprigs

Remove the rind from the bacon, cut each rasher into 2 or 3 pieces and make into small rolls, securing each with a cocktail pick. Place the rolls in a dry pan and cook until the bacon fat is clear. Lift out and keep hot.

Roll the chicken livers in seasoned flour and cook in the pan with the bacon fat for about 10 minutes. Lift out. Add about 1 tablespoon of seasoned flour

to the pan and stir until brown, then pour in the stock or water and stir until boiling. Add the mushrooms, soy sauce, and sherry with salt and pepper to taste. Replace the cooked livers in the hot gravy and cook for a few more minutes. Pile on to hot buttered toast, top with the bacon rolls and garnish with parsley sprigs. Serves 4–6.

CHICKEN LIVERS CONTINENTAL

Sauce
1½ tablespoons butter
1 clove garlic, minced
1 tablespoon minced onion
1½ tablespoons plain flour
1 cup beef stock or water and stock cube

Livers
¼ cup flour
½ teaspoon salt
Pinch pepper
1 tablespoon butter
500 g (1 lb) chicken livers
1½ tablespoons Madeira
Freshly boiled rice for serving

In a saucepan melt the butter for the sauce and add the garlic and onion. Cook, stirring constantly until the onion is soft but not brown. Blend in the flour and cook for a few minutes, again without browning, then add the stock and cook, stirring constantly until the sauce boils and thickens. Cover and let simmer while you cook the livers.

Combine the flour, salt and pepper and use to coat the livers. Melt the butter in a pan and quickly fry the livers until brown all over. Slowly pour in the Madeira and then the sauce. Cover and simmer for about 10 minutes. Serve over freshly cooked rice. Serves 4.

CHICKEN LIVER STROGANOFF

500 g (1 lb) chicken livers
Seasoned flour
2 tablespoons butter
1 small onion, peeled and chopped finely
250 g (½ lb) fresh mushrooms, sliced
¼ cup water
Salt and pepper
2 tablespoons fresh or cultured sour cream
Freshly boiled rice for serving

Trim the chicken livers into neat pieces and coat them with seasoned flour. Heat the butter in a pan and fry the livers gently until browned then remove from the pan. Add the onion and cook, stirring well until soft then add the mushrooms, water, salt and pepper. Stir until the mixture boils.

Return the livers to the pan, cover and simmer for

about 15 minutes. Stir in the cream and reheat without boiling. Serve over freshly boiled rice. Serves 4.

CURRIED LAMB PIES

2 teaspoons fat
1 teaspoon finely chopped onion
3 teaspoons plain flour
1 rounded teaspoon curry powder
Salt and pepper
1 soup cube
1 cup stock *or* water
1 cup chopped cooked lamb
½ an apple, diced
2 tablespoons coconut
Lemon juice
250 g (½ lb) flaky pastry
1 egg beaten with a little milk

Melt the fat in a saucepan, add the onion and cook until soft and brown. Add the flour and curry powder, and salt and pepper to taste. Cook for 1 minute. Dissolve the soup cube in the stock or water and add, stirring until the mixture boils and thickens. Add the lamb, peeled and diced apple, the coconut and a squeeze of lemon juice. Allow to cool.
Roll the pastry and cut some into rounds to line small patty tins, with smaller rounds to cover. Place one of the larger rounds in each patty tin and add a spoonful of the curried mixture to each. Glaze the edges and cover with a small round of pastry.
Make a small hole in the centre of each pie. Brush the tops with egg mixture. Bake in a hot oven, 230° C (450° F), for 15 or 20 minutes. Makes 12.

KIDNEY D'AMOUR

6 rashers bacon
9 sheeps' kidneys *or* 1½ ox kidneys
Seasoned flour
1 tablespoon chopped onion
1½ cups stock *or* 1½ cups water and soup cube
Salt and pepper
½ teaspoon mixed mustard
1 teaspoon lemon juice
1 teaspoon sugar
2 tablespoons sherry *or* port
3 eggs, scrambled
¼ teaspoon salt and a dash of pepper for eggs
4 tablespoons milk
1 tablespoon chopped parsley

Garnish: parsley sprigs

Remove the rind from the bacon and cut the rashers into small pieces. Roll each piece up and secure with cocktail picks. Fry lightly in a pan until the fat is clear.
Soak the kidneys in tepid water for 30 minutes. Drain and dry them and remove the white tubes, then slice and roll in seasoned flour.
Remove the bacon from the pan, add the kidney slices and fry lightly. Add the chopped onion and fry for a further 3 minutes, then add the stock, salt and pepper to taste, mustard, lemon juice and sugar. Stir until boiling. Cover and simmer for about 40 minutes (the time will depend on the thickness of the kidney slices).
Add the sherry or port, and thicken if necessary with a little blended flour.
Scramble the eggs with the salt, pepper, milk and chopped parsley. Place the cooked kidney on a hot serving dish and surround with the scrambled egg. Garnish with the bacon rolls and some parsley sprigs. Serves 6.

CHEESE AND KIDNEY CHARLOTTE

6 sheeps' kidneys *or* 1 ox kidney
1 good-sized onion, sliced
1½ cups cold water
½ teaspoon salt
¼ teaspoon pepper
1 teaspoon lemon juice
3 bacon rashers, rind removed
2 tablespoons plain flour
2 eggs
¾ cup milk
8 slices bread
1 cup grated tasty cheese

Garnish: parsley

Soak the kidneys for about 15 minutes in tepid water. Drain and dry, then remove the fine skin and white core. Chop finely and place in a saucepan with the onion, the cold water, salt, pepper and lemon juice, and the bacon rashers.
Cover and simmer until the kidney is tender. Take off the heat. Blend the flour with a little cold water and stir into the mixture, return the saucepan to the heat and cook, stirring well until the mixture boils. Cook for a further minute. Set aside.
Beat the eggs lightly and add the milk. Remove the crusts and cut each slice of bread in half then dip the pieces lightly into the egg and milk mixture, then into the grated cheese.
Line a buttered dish with some of the bread slices and spoon in the kidney mixture. Cover with the remaining bread slices and add any left-over cheese. Bake in a moderate oven, 180° C (350° F), for about 20 minutes or until the cheese on top has melted and cooked to a golden brown. Garnish with parsley and serve hot. Serves 4.

BEEF CHARLOTTE

4 rounded tablespoons bacon fat *or* margarine
10 slices bread
2 teaspoons margarine *or* butter for filling
1 medium-sized onion, chopped finely
500 g (1 lb) finely minced steak
½ teaspoon salt
Dash pepper
¾ cup tomato soup
2 tablespoons chopped parsley
2 tablespoons grated cheese

Melt the bacon fat or margarine in a saucepan. Remove the crusts and cut the bread into finger lengths. Brush each finger of bread on both sides with the melted fat or margarine. Use some of these fingers to line the bottom and sides of a 20 cm (8 in) tart plate. Keep the remainder for the top.
Melt the dessertspoon of margarine or butter in a pan, add the finely chopped onion and cook until soft but not brown. Add the minced steak and cook, stirring well until it changes colour. Add the salt, pepper, tomato soup and chopped parsley. When boiling, reduce the heat, cover and simmer for 10 minutes.
Pour into the lined tart plate, top with the remaining fingers of bread and sprinkle with the grated cheese. Bake in a hot oven, 220° C (425° F), for 20 minutes or until a golden brown. Serve immediately. Serves 4.

BEEF CROQUETTES

2 rashers bacon
250 g (½ lb) finely minced steak
1½ to 2 cups mashed potato
2 tablespoons finely chopped onion
1 tablespoon finely chopped parsley
Salt and pepper
Seasoned flour
Egg beaten with 1 tablespoon milk
Breadcrumbs
Fat *or* oil for frying

Garnish: tomato wedges and in-season vegetables

Sauté the bacon until crisp. Drain and dice. Add the meat to the fat left in the pan, and cook, stirring well until it changes colour. Combine with the mashed potato, onion, bacon and parsley and season to taste with salt and pepper. Chill well to make the mixture easier to handle.
Take spoonsful of the mixture and shape into croquettes or cork shapes in the seasoned flour. Coat each croquette with egg mixture before covering with the breadcrumbs. Deep-fry the croquettes until they are golden in colour, and drain on paper. Serve garnished with wedges of fresh tomato, accompanied by vegetables in season. Serves 4.

VEAL SALTIMBOCCA

8 thin slices veal
½ teaspoon finely rubbed sage
Seasoned pepper
8 thin slices prosciutto ham
Butter
2 tablespoons dry white wine
Croutons of fried bread

Using a meat mallet flatten the veal slices until they are about 10 cm (4 in) square. Add a little sage to each. Season with the pepper. Place a thin slice of the ham on each piece of veal, roll up and secure each one with a wooden toothpick.
Cook these rolls in the melted butter in a saucepan until they are brown on all sides, then add the wine. Cover and cook very slowly until the rolls are tender. This should only take about 15 minutes and it may be necessary to add a little more wine if it boils away. Remove the toothpicks and serve the veal accompanied with croutons of fried bread. Serves 4.

SWEETBREADS WITH ASPARAGUS AND PÂTÉ CREAM

1 kg (2 lb) veal sweetbreads
2 teaspoons lemon juice
2 teaspoons salt
Flour, seasoned
Salt and pepper
Egg glazing
Breadcrumbs
1½ tablespoons butter *or* oil
1 440 g (14 oz) can asparagus spears
1½ tablespoons dry vermouth
1 teaspoon mustard (Dijon style for preference)
½ cup whipping cream
1 90 g (3 oz) can liver pâté
Nutmeg, freshly grated

Garnish: lemon wedges

Soak the sweetbreads in cold water for about one hour. Drain and remove the skin. Place them in a saucepan with about five cups of water and add the salt and lemon juice. Cover, bring to the boil then simmer for 20 minutes. Drain, place between two plates with a weight on top and press until the sweetbreads are cold and set, preferably overnight.
Cut them into squares or break into clusters and toss them in seasoned flour. Dip each piece in egg glazing and then cover with breadcrumbs. Fry in oil or butter until golden all over then drain the sweetbreads on paper and keep hot. Drain the asparagus and sauté in the hot butter. Lift out and place with the sweetbreads. To the pan add the Vermouth, mustard and cream and stir to thoroughly mix. Cover and cook over a medium heat until the cream has reduced and thickened slightly. Remove from the heat and

add the pâté which has been cut into chunks. Stir until smooth. Taste, add salt if required then spoon the pâté cream to cover the sweetbreads and asparagus. Sprinkle lightly with freshly grated nutmeg and serve with lemon wedges. Serves 4–6.

FLAMBÉ OF KIDNEYS SUPREME

60 g (2 oz) butter
1 small onion, peeled and chopped
3 veal kidneys
125 g (4 oz) mushrooms, sliced
¼ cup brandy
Salt and pepper
1 cup cream
1 teaspoon mixed mustard
Parsley, chopped and toast fingers

Melt the butter in a fry pan, add the onion and cook until soft. Remove the white tubes and skin from the kidneys, slice, add with the mushrooms to the onions in the pan. Cook, turning the kidneys over gently, for about five minutes or until the kidneys lose their pink colour. Pour over the brandy, ignite it, and when the flame dies down season with salt and pepper.
Combine the cream with the mustard and pour over the kidneys. Cook, stirring lightly, until the cream is thoroughly heated. Serve immediately, lightly sprinkled with chopped parsley and accompanied by fingers of toast. Serves 4.

SAUTÉED VEAL KIDNEYS WITH MUSHROOMS

6 veal kidneys
Seasoned flour
1½ tablespoons butter
1 large onion or ½ bunch shallots, chopped
375 g (¾ lb) mushrooms, sliced
½ cup red wine
Plain flour
1 cup cooked tomatoes
1 tablespoon parsley, chopped

Trim away any fat from the kidneys, cut them into small pieces and toss in a mixture of flour, pepper and salt. Heat the butter in a pan, add the kidneys and cook slowly, turning them over and over as they cook, for about 10 minutes. Lift out and keep hot.
To the butter left in the pan (or add a little more if necessary) add the onion or shallot and cook until they are tender. Add mushrooms and toss until tender.
Sprinkle a scant tablespoon of flour into the pan and cook for a few minutes then add the wine, the cooked tomatoes and parsley. Stir until the sauce boils. Reduce it to a thicker consistency if necessary by boiling, then add the kidneys. Reheat and serve over toast points. Serves 6.

SAUSAGE AND TOMATO PIE

1 small onion, sliced
1 teaspoon butter or margarine
500 g (1 lb) pork sausages
2 large tomatoes, peeled and sliced
50 ml (¼ pt) stock or water
500 g (1 lb) potatoes, boiled and mashed
Milk
Butter

Fry onion in the teaspoon of butter or margarine until it is quite soft. Place the sausages in tepid water, bring to the boil, simmer for 5 minutes, then drain. Take off the skin, slice the sausages and place half of them in a shallow dish.
Place half tomato slices on top of the sausage, then add the onion. Season with salt and pepper and add the stock or water, then the remaining slices of sausage and the rest of the sliced tomato.
Spread a thick layer of mashed potato over the top, brush with milk and dot with small pieces of butter. Score the surface with the back of a knife.
Bake in a hot oven, 200° C (400° F), until the potato topping is a golden brown. Serves 4.

SAUSAGE AND EGG CASSEROLE

500 g (1 lb) pork sausage mince
4 hard-boiled eggs
2 tablespoons butter
¼ cup plain flour
½ teaspoon salt
Pinch pepper
2 cups milk
1 440 g (14 oz) can whole kernel corn
2 tablespoons chopped parsley
1 cup buttered breadcrumbs

Garnish: parsley

Brown the pork sausage mince and drain it of any fat.
Remove the shells from the eggs, slice 2 of them and place in a well-greased 6 cup capacity casserole. Melt the butter in a saucepan, add the flour and stir until smooth, then cook for 1 minute without browning. Season with the salt and pepper, then add the milk and stir until the sauce boils and thickens. Stir in the well-drained corn and parsley, and simmer for 3 minutes.
Pour half the sauce over the sliced eggs in the casserole and arrange the browned and drained pork mince on top. Cover with the rest of the sauce. Slice the remaining eggs and place on top, then sprinkle with buttered breadcrumbs.
Bake at 190° C (375° F) for 20 to 25 minutes or until the crumbs are brown and the filling heated through. Garnish with parsley. Serves 4.

BRAIN AND WALNUT PIES

3 sets cooked brains
1½ cups medium thick white sauce
60 g (2 oz) cooked ham
½ cup chopped walnuts
250 g (½ lb) flaky pastry

Cut the brains into small pieces and mix with the sauce. Add chopped ham and walnuts.

Roll the pastry thinly and cut some into rounds to line small patty cases. Cut an equal number of rounds a little smaller to cover the pies.

Place a spoonful of the brain mixture in each lined patty case, glaze the edges with water and cover with a smaller round of pastry. Make a hole in the top of each to allow the steam to escape. Bake in a hot oven, 230° C (450° F), for about 20 minutes. Serves 4–6.

BRAIN CAKES

2 sets cooked brains
3 teaspoons butter
3 level tablespoons plain flour
½ teaspoon salt
Pinch cayenne pepper
Pinch nutmeg
1 cup milk
1 hard-boiled egg, chopped
Seasoned flour
1 egg beaten with 1 tablespoon milk
Breadcrumbs
Fat or oil for frying
Bacon rolls or tomato wedges

Garnish: parsley sprigs

Cut the well-chilled cooked brains into 1 cm (½ in) pieces. Melt the butter in a saucepan, add the flour and stir until smooth, then cook for 1 minute without browning. Flavour with the salt, cayenne and nutmeg. Add the milk and stir until the sauce boils and thickens—it will be very thick.

Fold in the chopped brains and chopped egg and turn on to a plate to become quite cold. Take spoonsful of the mixture and shape into round flat cakes in seasoned flour. Dip each cake in the egg and milk mixture, then cover with breadcrumbs. Deep-fry in hot fat or oil until a golden brown, then drain on paper.

Serve with grilled bacon rolls or wedges of fresh tomato. Add a garnish of parsley sprigs. Serves 4.

BRAINS ITALIAN STYLE

4 sets cooked brains
2 slightly beaten eggs
2 teaspoons cold water
½ teaspoon grated Parmesan cheese
½ teaspoon chopped parsley
¼ teaspoon salt
Pinch pepper
Breadcrumbs
Oil for frying

Sauce

1 tablespoon butter
3 cups sliced tomatoes
2 stalks celery, chopped
1 slice onion
1 bayleaf
1 tablespoon cornflour
½ teaspoon salt
Pinch pepper
½ teaspoon sugar
Water or stock

Cut the brains into quarters. Blend the beaten eggs, water, cheese, parsley, salt and pepper.

Dip the pieces of brain in this mixture, then roll them in breadcrumbs. Fry in hot oil until a golden brown on all sides, then drain on paper. Serve with the tomato sauce.

To make the sauce melt the butter in a saucepan and fry the tomato slices, chopped celery, slice of onion and bayleaf until soft. Cover and simmer for 15 minutes, then press through a sieve. Blend the cornflour with the salt, pepper, sugar and a little water or stock, add to the tomato purée and stir over medium heat until the sauce boils and thickens. Simmer for 2 minutes before serving. Serves 4.

BRAIN AND TOMATO SAVOURY

2 sets sheeps brains
Water
Salt
Bay leaf or mace
1 teaspoon butter
1 medium-sized tomato
Pinch cayenne pepper
1 teaspoon instant onion
1 cup thick white sauce
Buttered toast

Soak the brains in cold water for about 30 minutes. Remove the skin. Place in a saucepan, cover with cold water and bring to the boil. Drain. Replace with cold water containing a little salt and a bay leaf or a piece of mace. Cover, bring to the boil and cook for about nine minutes. Drain.

Melt the butter in a small saucepan and add the chopped tomato, pepper and onion. Sauté for a few minutes or till both the onion and tomato are soft. Add the white sauce and stir until blended. Cut the brains into 2.5 cm (1 in) pieces and fold into the hot sauce mixture. Spoon on to slices of hot buttered toast. Serves 2–3.

MOCK CHICKEN FRICASSÉE

750 g (1½ lb) tripe
2 teaspoons salt
2 large white onions, whole
1 packet chicken noodle soup
½ cup milk
2 tablespoons plain flour blended with a little cold milk
2 teaspoons butter
Pinch cayenne pepper
1 tablespoon chopped parsley

Wash the tripe and cut it into 1 cm (½ in) squares. Place in a saucepan, cover with cold water and bring to the boil. Drain. Add the salt and onions, cover with fresh cold water, and simmer for 2 hours or until the tripe is tender.
Remove all but 1½ cups of the cooking liquid. Lift out the onions, chop them finely then replace in the saucepan with the tripe. Add the chicken noodle soup and the milk and simmer for 10 minutes.
Add the blended flour to the contents of the saucepan and stir until the mixture comes to the boil, then cook for 3 minutes. Add the butter, cayenne and chopped parsley. Serve with triangles of dry toast. Serves 4.

TRIPE AND TOMATO PIE

3 tablespoons butter *or* margarine
3 level tablespoons plain flour
½ teaspoon salt
¼ teaspoon of pepper
2 cups milk
125 g (4 oz) bacon
3 tomatoes, sliced thinly
1 kg (2 lb) cooked tripe cut into 2.5 cm (1 in) squares
1 egg
2 cups mashed potato
2 tablespoons grated cheese for topping

Melt the butter in a saucepan, add the flour, salt and pepper, and stir until smooth. Cook for another minute without browning, then add the milk and stir and cook until the sauce boils and thickens.
Lightly fry or grill the bacon, then cut it into small pieces. Skin and thinly slice the tomatoes.
Stir the cooked tripe squares into the sauce and pour half into a lightly greased casserole. Add half the bacon and tomatoes, then the remainder of the tripe, sauce, bacon and tomatoes.
Add the beaten egg to the mashed potato and spread over the top of the mixture in the casserole. Score the surface with a fork and sprinkle with grated cheese. Bake in a hot oven, 220° C (425° F), for about 15 minutes. Serves 4–6.

INDEX